SUPERTEAMS

'Khoi Tu has an inspirational mind, full of curiosity, and a strong desire
to find solutions for issues that can seem to be unsolvable'
Sir Jackie Stewart, three-time World Drivers' Champion

'Products, companies and organizations that are brilliant, fun and
deliver on their promise often look super-simple to the outside world,
but the detail and speed happening behind the scenes is frightening.
To achieve this, let alone keep it going, requires the right team and leadership, good, solid relationships, plus a little bit of magic. For me this is
what this book is all about – it shows what people can do in different
scenarios, especially when the going gets tough and there's a goal
to be achieved. Nice one, Khoi' Jamie Oliver

ABOUT THE AUTHOR

Khoi Tu is a leadership and teamwork consultant who has worked with teams at Coca-Cola, BP, Deutsche Bank, UBS, Tesco, LVMH and the British Red Cross. He has also advised some of the world's most influential individuals, including Jamie Oliver, and Formula One world champions. A graduate of the London School of Economics, he worked around the world for Shell before joining the pioneering web design company Razorfish. In 2006 he started his own company, Inverstar.

Khoi Tu will donate all his royalties from the sale of *Superteams* to the British Red Cross, which works both in the UK and overseas.

SUPERTEAMS
How to Take Your Team to the Top!

Khoi Tu

PORTFOLIO
PENGUIN

PORTFOLIO PENGUIN

Published by the Penguin Group
Penguin Books Ltd, 80 Strand, London WC2R ORL, England
Penguin Group (USA) Inc., 375 Hudson Street, New York, New York 10014, USA
Penguin Group (Canada), 90 Eglinton Avenue East, Suite 700, Toronto, Ontario, Canada M4P 2Y3
(a division of Pearson Penguin Canada Inc.)
Penguin Ireland, 25 St Stephen's Green, Dublin 2, Ireland (a division of Penguin Books Ltd)
Penguin Group (Australia), 707 Collins Street, Melbourne, Victoria 3008, Australia
(a division of Pearson Australia Group Pty Ltd)
Penguin Books India Pvt Ltd, 11 Community Centre, Panchsheel Park, New Delhi – 110 017, India
Penguin Group (NZ), 67 Apollo Drive, Rosedale, Auckland 0632, New Zealand
(a division of Pearson New Zealand Ltd)
Penguin Books (South Africa) (Pty) Ltd, Block D, Rosebank Office Park,
181 Jan Smuts Avenue, Parktown North, Gauteng 2193, South Africa

Penguin Books Ltd, Registered Offices: 80 Strand, London WC2R ORL, England

www.penguin.com

First published by Portfolio Penguin 2012
Published in this edition 2014
001

Typeset by Jouve (UK), Milton Keynes
Printed in Great Britain by Clays Ltd, St Ives plc

ISBN: 978–0–241–95979–4

www.greenpenguin.co.uk

Penguin Books is committed to a sustainable
future for our business, our readers and our planet.
This book is made from Forest Stewardship
Council™ certified paper.

CONTENTS

'I honestly believe that none of us are as strong individually as we are collectively.'

Ronnie Wood

INTRODUCTION

The idea for this book began to form while I was working as a strategy and leadership consultant with some inspiring individuals, including world champion Formula 1 drivers and the leaders of some of the largest and most successful organizations in the world.

I am fascinated by such people. What qualities do these individuals possess that enable them to achieve so much? In my experience, there is no question they have something special. What stands out first and foremost is their sense of purpose, determination and self-belief – as Muhammad Ali put it, champions must have the skill, but the will has to be stronger than the skill.

However, as I spent more time with them, another pattern emerged. Their success came, I realized, from more than simply their individual brilliance. The myth of the single hero is just that: a myth. Even the Lone Ranger had Tonto. On stage, in the boardroom or on the racetrack, what makes superstars so super is the amplification of their individual brilliance by a great team. Their interaction with a team made the crucial difference.

An F1 driver can be instinctively quick, but finish down the field in a poorly designed car running the wrong race strategy. And while the image of James Bond single-handedly saving the world captures our imagination, the reality is that the most urgent and daring missions are executed by teams of elite soldiers, hand-picked and specially trained. In the aftermath of disaster, individual acts of humanity can save lives and restore dignity. Organized in the right way, these individual acts can combine to save a country.

Most challenges of consequence require a collective response. Individual excellence is both necessary and critical, but the skill and the will to build, lead and perform in a team is often the difference between success and failure. Even for individual stars, failing to work effectively in a team can be a career-limiting flaw. In an interconnected world, the inability to be a good team player can have the same effect as kryptonite on Superman.

Even if this seems self-evident, it is easier said than done. Great teams are rare, and even fewer remain great for long. Most of us have experienced the thrill and camaraderie that result from working in synchronicity with others, but we have also had to endure endless unproductive meetings, destructive conflicts and a niggling sense that our colleagues are simply not trying as hard as we are, yet are getting more favourable treatment.

The aim of this book is to explore and unravel the inner workings of some great and high-performing teams – seven

'Superteams' – and through that to show how you can build your own better teams.

I chose each team at one important moment in its history, to try to uncover specific insights that can be translated into practical action.

My first Superteam is Pixar, a film studio that has had an unrivalled run of box office success, unique in an industry known for many releases but few hits. The Pixar team succeeded by fusing diverse skills and very different, often difficult personalities (including Steve Jobs) around a common purpose.

I then turn to golf, specifically to the 2010 European Ryder Cup team. How did the captain, Colin Montgomerie, construct a winning team comprising twelve players usually characterized by their intense rivalry?

The armed forces provide the personnel for the next team. The SAS is the blueprint for special forces around the world. Tracing the story leading up to the freeing of the hostages held by terrorists during the 1980 Iranian embassy siege in London offers insights for all teams into how to select and train for great results.

In a closely associated though almost polar opposite field, my work with Sir Nicholas Young and his team at the British Red Cross, and my experience of their purposeful professionalism in action, was one of the main inspirations for this book. (Indeed, all the royalties from its sales will go to support their vital work.) Their response to the Haiti earthquake epitomizes the idea that teamwork can change the world for the better.

The idea that the stars that burn brightest tend to burn out quickest is often used to explain the failure of many bands to survive beyond their first album. The story of the Rolling Stones shines a light on how to burn brightly for fifty years as the greatest rock 'n' roll band in the world.

Superteams don't always start out that way. The collection of leaders who drove the Northern Ireland peace process became a team, despite starting out as sworn enemies holding diametrically opposed views. Their story is a triumph of the politics of peace and also offers valuable lessons in how to master intra-team conflict.

Finally comes the Ferrari F1 team during their journey back from two decades of underachievement to the front of the Formula 1 grid. Their experience highlights how teams can overcome the many challenges of change to find success.

In submerging myself within these seven stories I learned many new things about teams. The research, including discussions with many of the team members themselves, was enlightening. The findings, included in the 'Team Talk' section of each chapter, challenged some of the myths of teams, as well as validating many of the tried and tested approaches I have used.

While each of the teams covered in the book is both 'super' and unique, the lessons they teach can be applied much more widely. The 'Agenda' that follows each story is designed for action, setting out a way for you to build and be part of a high-performing team.

Every team is different, but the shared secret of teamwork

is that it has to be worked at. Becoming a better team requires that you ask difficult questions, make tough choices and take action. I hope that this book will make the route clearer and easier, inspiring and guiding you and your team to greater success.

'There was so much trust between us. We all had slightly different talents and there was immense respect for what each person brought to the collaboration. It doesn't matter whose idea it is. We use the one that makes the movie better.'

John Lasseter

1
PIXAR
The power of common purpose

**'Black Friday' – 19 November 1993,
Walt Disney Co., Burbank, California**

Pixar are in production on their first full-length feature film, Toy Story, *green-lighted by Disney in 1992. The opportunity to make the movie represents the culmination of decades of pioneering and loss-making R&D by Pixar in the field of computer animation. The early stages of the* Toy Story *production have been characterized by the movie novices in the Pixar team yielding to the expertise of the Disney studio and especially the company's powerful head, Jeffrey Katzenberg. At the screening of the first half of the film the consensus across both the Pixar and Disney teams is that the film is terrible. In working hard to placate Katzenberg and give the film an edge intended to ensure it will appeal to children, teenagers and adults, the Pixar team have lost sight of their own movie. Even Woody, the central character, has turned into a complete jerk, too unlikeable to capture an audience's emotions. Disney orders a shutdown of the production, threatening major layoffs. But Pixar founder and head of animation John Lasseter successfully pleads for a two-week reprieve.*

When John Lasseter secured that fortnight's extension for his Pixar team to forge a new version of *Toy Story*, under immense physical and mental stress, his sole focus was fighting for the survival of the movie and the company he believed in passionately.

He had no idea that this crisis would turn what was a very good team into a great team. They already had a shared vision, a mutual understanding of what they all considered to be good, a passion for technology and art, and a belief in the prime importance of storytelling. But the enormity of this moment of challenge was the trigger which allowed Pixar to become a superteam. They had no option but to rely on mutual accountability, to learn how to criticize each other quickly and constructively.

In the crucible of adversity they developed processes and ways of operating that proved so successful that in the aftermath of the crisis the Pixar team strove to retain those processes as part of their daily work, to turn principles and practices into a way of life.

> 'It was really very scary and I think that's where we bonded as a group. It was do or die time: the Grim Reaper was in the room, standing in the corner. It was like, "OK, you guys. If this story does not work, the whole project, the whole place is dead!"'
>
> Story writer Joe Ranft

Composition: the best diverse talent

The core team that created Pixar – Ed Catmull, Alvy Ray Smith, John Lasseter and Steve Jobs – are proof that the starting point of superteams is great individual talent. The only time brilliant, super-creative individuals will share the same room is when they have a common purpose. In Pixar's case, the talent was united by a shared belief that it was possible to create cinematic magic using cutting-edge animation technology.

The origins of Pixar, however, owed much to other legendary teams in the technological world, the first of which was Xerox PARC – which had a direct and lasting impact on Steve Jobs. To understand the Pixar story, you have to understand the Steve Jobs story.

In 1970, Xerox founded the Palo Alto Research Center (PARC) as a research facility in the burgeoning area of digital technology. It became a legendary incubation centre for much of modern computing and was responsible for helping to develop both the computer mouse and the graphical user interface (GUI) that for the first time allowed software users to 'point and click' as opposed to typing in commands. It was a hothouse of creative and technical geniuses, including Alan Kay, who worked on the GUI and object-orientated programming, Butler Lampson, a major contributor to the 'what-you-see-is-what-you-get' (WYSIWYG) text editor, and Charles Thacker, co-inventor with Bob Metcalfe of the

Ethernet local area networking system. Metcalfe went on to found 3Com, a networking equipment company, which he later sold to Hewlett Packard for $2.7 billion.

PARC had famous commercial successes of its own, laser printing proving one of the most profitable lines for Xerox, but is also infamous for the ones that got away. The company combined many of the innovations to form the basis of one of the world's first personal computers, the Alto. This was not a success for Xerox but it provided an inspiration, not only in terms of ideas but also how to improve them, for another computer pioneer: Steve Jobs at Apple. Jobs had offered Xerox the opportunity to invest in Apple if he could have access to the developments at PARC. In return for an option to buy $1 million of Apple stock in the company's second round of financing, in December 1979 Xerox opened the kimono to Jobs and his fledgling team. What they saw changed the game for personal technology for ever.

Jobs was fond of quoting Picasso's line that good artists borrow and great artists steal. A year on, Xerox had made a $16 million profit on its Apple shares. The mouse and GUI that Jobs and his team had seen at PARC gave them the basis to make the breakthroughs that were to become central elements of the user experience that have since been the vital edge of Apple's success.

By 1983, having successfully improved upon PARC's innovations, Jobs had lured John Sculley from PepsiCo to Apple, having offered him the choice of changing the world or spending the rest of his life selling cola. Jobs saw in Sculley a potential mentor, a father figure to replace the one he hardly knew. Sculley was flattered and thought he could be a great teacher to this brilliant student. He came in as CEO above Jobs as head of the Macintosh division. The early relationship was happy and symbiotic, the two men feeding off each other.

But the brilliant Jobs also had a dark side. He was ruthless and dismissive of others and consumed by his own projects, rather than by the whole firm. Apple co-founder Steve Wozniak left the company, citing difficulties in getting the focus on the second-generation Apple II computer, as Jobs was hoarding the attention and resources for his Macintosh baby.

Wozniak was widely seen as a cuddly genius whose biggest weakness was his generosity and community spirit. He sold at very low prices chunks of his own stake to many of the early staffers at Apple who weren't part of the hundreds made millionaires by the IPO, so that they too could profit from the company going public. On leaving Apple, Wozniak hired the same design firm as Apple to work on his new product: a remote control device. Despite the fact that the two were not in competition, Jobs took legal action to prevent the design firm from working with Wozniak. It was an uncomfortable end to a productive partnership between the two Apple founders. As Wozniak commented soon afterwards, 'Steve can be an insulting and hurtful guy.'

The honeymoon between John Sculley and Steve Jobs also faltered. In reality Jobs did not want a mentor, certainly not one he considered less brilliant than he was where it mattered. He was prone to projecting the image of the perfect coach on to people and then becoming contemptuous of them when they failed to live up to his expectations. On his side, Sculley found Jobs' rudeness – what the marketing chief at Apple called his 'management by character assassination' – hard to bear. He wondered if the mood swings and rebellious behaviour resulted from more than immaturity, perhaps even something clinical.

The souring of the early romance was accelerated with disagreements on issues of substance. The arguments over pricing and launching the Macintosh were particularly painful, as they highlighted differences in both vision and values. For Jobs, keeping the price low and making a big splash were central to his passion for the product and his vision of changing the world by democratizing computing. Sculley was adamant the product had to be more expensive to reflect the costs of marketing; from his point of view, the product, no matter how revolutionary, still needed to make a healthy profit.

After the seminal Orwellian-themed advert for the 1984 Macintosh launch (in which the Mac was portrayed as saving the world from 'Big Brother' computing conformity), sales peaked and then slowed dramatically. Jobs blamed Sculley's behaviour, and particularly his pricing decisions. He became increasingly erratic, with ever greater numbers of Apple staff and even partners caught in his ruthless put-downs. Sculley also came under fire from the Apple board, for not taking stronger action to manage Jobs' destructive streak. Compelled to act, and with the board's backing, he promoted Jobs out of the way, giving him a role as chairman and global visionary. Given a big title clearly shorn of power, Jobs had no executive or operational control. He had no choice but to leave.

Bitter and disappointed, he sold all but one of his 6.5 million Apple shares, representing 11 per cent of the company's total stock. It gave him no pleasure that news of his resignation had pushed the shares up 7 per cent and got him a much better price. To add to the acrimony of the divorce from the company he had founded, Apple sued him after he was joined by six other Apple employees to start his new computer venture, NeXT.

> 'What I'm best at doing is finding a group of talented people and making things with them.'
> Steve Jobs

During the summer of 1985, just as he was leaving Apple, Steve Jobs went for a walk with Alan Kay, whom he had recruited from PARC the previous year to become an Apple Fellow. Kay introduced him to one group of extremely talented people: Ed Catmull, Alvy Ray Smith and John Lasseter.

Kay had first met Ed Catmull at the University of Utah in the early 1970s. Utah, like PARC, was a hotbed of technological innovation. Kay's and Catmull's contemporaries there included Jim Clark, who went on to co-found Silicon Graphics and Netscape, and John Warnock, a co-founder of Adobe.

Ed Catmull had originally wanted to work as an animator at the Disney Studios, but while he was at high school he felt he did not possess the technical draughtsmanship he would need and refocused on computer programming. His secret passion was using computers to make animation at a time when computer animation was still at the 'lunatic fringe' of technology. While at Utah he invented three pioneering techniques to drive computer animation: bi-cubic patches, z-buffering and texture mapping, each one revolutionary and legendary. Reserved, unassuming, respectful, a strict Mormon, he took two years out from his studies to gain missionary experience and, after failing to become a teacher, found himself in a dead-end software job.

Alvy Ray Smith was passionate about painting and had exhibited his art. He supported his passion by working in computer programming and technology, particularly cellular automation, the field of self-reproducing machines. He had dropped out as he became convinced that his work was supporting military aims. An outgoing, outspoken Texan turned Californian hippie, Ray Smith had also worked at the Xerox PARC innovation centre, developing a colour paint project. The project was cancelled when Xerox decided the future of business printing was black and white. Alvy Ray Smith was fired.

Both Catmull and Ray Smith had ended up at the new Computer Graphics Lab at the New York Institute of Technology, leading research into computer graphics and animation. Their work there in the late 1970s attracted the attention of George Lucas, who was looking to capitalize on the success of *Star Wars* and wanted to explore bringing computer graphics into his future films. In 1984, as part of Lucasfilm's computer graphics division, they recruited a young animator recently fired from Disney.

John Lasseter had always loved cartoons and animation. At fourteen, in ninth grade, he came across Bob Thomas' *The Art of Animation*, a history of Disney Studios and the making of *Sleeping Beauty*. He realized that animation could be a career, and after watching *The Sword in the Stone* declared he wanted to work at Walt Disney. He was an early graduate of Cal Arts, the Disney animation school; his fellow students included future heavyweights like Tim Burton, John Musker (co-director of *Aladdin*, *The Little Mermaid* and *Hercules*), Chris Buck (director of *Tarzan*) and Brad Bird (director of *Iron Giant* and *The Incredibles*).

John, an ebullient storyteller, was quickly recognized as supertalented – he picked up a student Oscar for his early work – and after working at the Disney theme parks joined the Disney animation team. But the Walt Disney company culture had drifted away from its founders' original spirit of marrying technology and art with masterful storytelling. Even animation was now regarded as tangential to the company's strategy. While Walt had been a collector of talent, Lasseter was now regarded as a cultural misfit. Caught in the crossfire between two feuding bosses, Lasseter was fired, free to join Catmull and Ray Smith at Lucasfilm.

By the time Steve Jobs was introduced to the team of three at Lucasfilm he already shared a common web of experiences with them. They had all operated at the highest levels of their respective fields; they shared a profound respect for both scientific and artistic innovation; they had each come from small groups surrounded by other gifted engineers and creatives. All four of them had been fired from organizations that had become incompatible with their passions. Most importantly, they remained passionate about the possibilities at the intersection of creativity and technology.

> 'I realized they were way ahead of others in combining art and technology, which is what I've always been interested in.'
>
> Steve Jobs

True to his beliefs Jobs backed his ability to see an opportunity and to spot talent. He invested $5 million to buy the graphics division from Lucasfilm and $5 million to capitalize it effectively. Over the following years up to 1991 he invested a further $55 million in the loss-making Pixar, keeping his faith in the capabilities of the team.

It seemed a perfect team composition, a meeting of minds with their common heritage. Indeed, over the years the team settled into naturally distinctive roles that played to their strengths and interests. Steve Jobs focused on the big picture and doing key deals, Ed Catmull concentrated on operational management and technical development while John Lasseter led on creativity and story.

The core members of the Pixar team proved that getting the team mix right was essential. George Lucas once observed that Ed Catmull, above and beyond his talent for writing software, had a secret passion for making movies. John Lasseter, on the other hand, was a brilliant animating genius, with his own secret passion: computer animation. 'It was a marriage made in heaven,' Lucas remarked.

But, as Sculley had discovered, individuals who could invent the future, and who had the charisma and audacity to sell it to the world, were rarely the easiest to work with. Those maverick entrepreneurs prepared to take on the status quo armed with little more than their own ingenuity are edgy to start with. With a lot of success and good doses of failure they can become extreme.

In many respects Alvy Ray Smith and Steve Jobs were too similar. They were passionate and driven, both with big egos and neither prepared to back down. Alvy reacted badly to the dark side of the Jobs personality. The reality distortion field that worked its magic on many pushed the wrong buttons with him. Not surprisingly, the interaction was too explosive. A nose-to-nose shouting match over the use of a whiteboard was the final straw. Ray Smith may have been able to shout as loudly but Jobs owned 70 per cent of the company. Ray Smith left the team, eventually setting up his own firm, Altamira Software Corporation, which he sold to Microsoft in 1994, becoming their first Graphics Fellow the same year.

Jobs, like other leading minds in technology, and especially amongst those who started their own businesses, was clear about the importance of great talent. He could not stand having to work with 'bozos' and would berate them directly for being 'shitheads who suck', but he could also be respectful of excellence. Nathan Myhrvold, former chief technology officer at Microsoft, put it succinctly: 'The difference between a great programmer and an average one was not five times, not a hundred, but ten thousand times.' The scalability of software meant that one great piece of code, one extraordinary algorithm, could revolutionize an entire industry. With the mass manufacture of personal computing the same was true for product design, as Jobs later proved with the ubiquity of the iPod. For Jobs and his cohort it was all down to the quality of the talent.

Steve Jobs respected Ed Catmull's engineering credentials, acknowledging the quality of the hardware and software he had developed. Importantly, Catmull's calm demeanour worked better with Jobs; he had an ability to go with the flow, bending in the wind like bamboo in the face of Jobs' 'tornado of ideas' but not breaking. He did not necessarily buy into everything that Jobs came up with. In particular Catmull never let go of his dream of making a computer-animated movie. Jobs was intent on recreating the Macintosh by translating the industrial hardware and software that Pixar pioneered and once again on a mission to make it mainstream.

Steve Jobs' relationship with John Lasseter was more supportive. Jobs saw in Lasseter an artist, someone with whom he could share his passion for design. He recognized Lasseter as one of the geniuses that he wanted to make tools for. They shared a deep desire to make things perfect, an obsession for quality that was uncomfortable with short cuts or mediocrity. But there were important differences, too; differences that made them work well together.

Where Jobs paid homage to minimalism, in his black polo neck with an Issey Miyake aesthetic, Lasseter sported bright Hawaiian shirts in an office filled with his giant toy collection. While Lasseter was as driven as Jobs, he demonstrated it in a different way, less effusive and sharp than Jobs, gentle and fun, nurturing his team rather than challenging them. It was a relationship similar to the one Jobs developed with the British designer Jonathan Ive, head of design at Apple, the man credited with the instantly covetable sleek look of Apple's products, from the iPod to the MacBook. Jobs recognized the power of making technology brilliantly functional and extraordinarily emotive. He respected both Ive's and Lasseter's ability to make digital products and characters which were technologically game-changing as well as sexy and loveable.

As Jobs built his team at Pixar, John Lasseter began to do the same, with equally exacting standards. Ed Catmull remembers that, 'unlike some people, who in a similar position might have hired people who were non-threatening, John had the confidence to bring really top-notch people into the company to become part of the core creative group. He sought out the very best people he could find. John has something of a magic touch for finding great people.'

One of the first people that Lasseter hired was Andrew

Stanton, who went on to script many of Pixar's films. Another early hire was Peter Doctor, who in Ed Catmull's view is 'one of the best animators in the world'.

In movie-making, as in most human endeavour, superior talent is often the telling advantage, the distinctive element that separates the sublime from the ordinary. The challenges of making a great movie require superior skills in many different areas – as highlighted by the length and diversity of the end production credits, from producers, directors, superstar cast and jobbing extras, to best boys and grips, accountants, lawyers and insurance specialists. From Pixar's perspective there was also the significant addition of the technologists, inventing as they went.

In Jobs, Catmull and Lasseter, Pixar had the highest calibre talent in every role. Importantly, they had enough in common but also enough diversity to be a truly magical mix.

The alchemy of teamwork at Pixar

For many good teams superior talent is necessary; for great teams, though, it is insufficient. The central challenge of becoming a great team is to harness the full range of talent in the team; to make the whole greater than the sum of the parts and to know when 'we' beats 'I' and when 'I' matters more than 'we'.

Pixar had no shortage of diverse talent. The real task was to forge an effective team from this collection of driven individuals. The first part of binding the group into something greater than the sum of the parts was the development of a common purpose.

Even film-makers like George Lucas saw only limited applications for computer animation, and did not believe the computer division should be making movies. He saw them as a support service for the director's vision. When John Lasseter was hired by Lucas, he was given the job title 'interface designer', rather than animator. This was partly because within Hollywood the first wave of computer graphics had seriously under-delivered and there was scepticism that it would prove just a flash in the pan.

Initially Jobs too saw Pixar as a graphics firm, like Apple, selling tools for the genius that would put a dent in the universe. He saw their product as hardware and software. The company name, Pixar, chosen after the acquisition from Lucas, came from one of the key graphics computers the firm was building. For several years after Pixar's creation, Lasseter's main function was to develop short movies to showcase the company's software and hardware.

It took two short movies – *Luxo Jr* and *Tin Toy* – to shift Steve Jobs' vision. As Jobs watched *Luxo Jr* – a story of the relationship between father and child standard lamps – at its premiere at the 1986 SIGGRAPH computer graphics convention in Dallas, a light went on, both on the screen and in his mind. In 1988 *Tin Toy* picked up an Oscar, the first time a computer-animated short had won an Academy Award. The story was a precursor to the full-length *Toy Story*, about the love between children and their toys. The impact of the story, the art and emotions powered by computer technology, how insanely great the movie was, shifted Jobs' perspective far more than John Sculley had been able to in his time trying to be Jobs' mentor.

Jobs admitted privately that his bet on Pixar's hardware and software business being rapidly adopted by consumers was wrong. The future of the firm lay in computer animation.

The team were now united by a shared vision, a common purpose: to marry technology and animation to create magic. They talked about nothing else. They set themselves – and each other – the highest of ambitions and standards. Few people and certainly not their original heroes in animation at Disney thought there was any real future in computer animation. So the vision of the team to be a movie company bound them together even tighter, against the rest of the world.

> 'The goal of the company and really the bliss of the company was to create a movie. That was the common dream.'
>
> Chuck Kolstad, former president of Pixar

From this point the entire team was aiming to become the new Disney. They all wanted to develop a new way of telling stories, by making movies in virtual worlds of mathematical constructions that could be at least as good as existing animation techniques, and then go beyond what those traditional techniques could do.

The Pixar team were prepared to be audacious. Ed Catmull and his team estimated that they would need to generate images containing 80 million polygons to be able to compete with film. This was an absurd number, given that the highest number of polygons even the most powerful computing power of the day could handle was only 500,000. 'Setting the bar at 80 million encouraged an entirely different sort of ambition and long-term thinking. It changed the whole mindset of problems we were trying to solve,' said Tom Porter, computer graphics innovator and associate producer at Pixar.

Smells like team spirit

The team at Pixar made a determined effort to develop a 'fraternity of geeks', as video graphics designer Ralph Guggenheim dubbed it. This was based on the same spirit that Ed Catmull had experienced at the University of Utah: 'Tackling a shared problem brings energy into the group of people and gives you a sense of camaraderie. Here was a whole community of people trying to solve the problems of computer graphics, writing papers and exchanging ideas. The whole field was moving forward with great excitement. That sense of community was so strong that it inspired me to try and recreate it after I left.'

And it was the same spirit that existed at Cal Arts, when John Lasseter was there. His fellow student John Musker remembers, 'We had a system at Cal Arts where we looked at each other's work. We were each other's critics and support-ers. We drew ideas from each other.'

Jobs' experiences at Apple and what he saw at Xerox PARC clearly played its part. He and the team were also influenced by the Northern Californian counterculture of the 1960s; Jobs often stated that drugs and particularly LSD had changed his life.

The boomerang-shaped Stanford Artificial Intelligence building, hidden up in the hills above Palo Alto, was the setting for a heady mix of programming breakthroughs, mari-juana and incense. Across those hills at the same time was the Stanford Research Institute, home to computer pioneer Douglas Engelbart, whose philosophy for changing the world influenced many who worked with him and who later went on to Xerox PARC. Engelbart believed that making the world a better place would require some form of organized effort. Harnessing humanity's collective IQ would dramatically improve the world's ability to solve problems, and computers would be essential to it.

With his colleagues at SRI Engelbart set out to build the computing technology to connect the world so it could resolve the most urgent problems. His inventions were highlighted in the 1968 'mother of all demos' at the Joint Computer Conference in San Francisco. The presentation of his research into Augmenting Human Intellect was a ninety-minute live demonstration that captivated the audience packing out the hall. Instead of standing at a podium, Engelbart was seated at a custom-designed console, where he drove his presentation via his NLS computer, residing thirty miles away in his research lab at Stanford Research Institute, on to a large projection screen overhead, flipping seamlessly between his presentation outline and a live demo of features, while video-teleconferencing members of his research lab lined in from SRI in shared-screen mode to demonstrate more of the system.

The impact of Engelbart's philosophy and that demonstration can still be felt today. The influence was there in every one of Steve Jobs' famed Apple product launches. The early ideas for the mouse began at SRI, travelled to PARC and then journeyed to the Macintosh. His original work on networked systems evolved in his development of the ARPANET, the first version of the internet. Most profoundly, his idea of using technology to connect and improve the world became the rallying cry for geeks across Silicon Valley and beyond.

It was the underlying spirit for the team, the 'fraternity of geeks' at Pixar. Together the experiences from across the team shaped their belief in a culture anchored in a team of peers, all contributing and sharing as many ideas as possible to use technology to change the world.

Beyond the marriage of technology and animation and the efforts to nurture the right creative culture, the Pixar team grew to understand the fundamental importance of story in making great films. Working at the New York Institute of Technology in 1975, Catmull and Ray Smith had helped produce a computer-animated film called *Tubby the Tuba*. While innovative from a technology perspective, the film was seen as a failure, primarily in terms of the plot and lack of direction. Overcoming this, Catmull and Ray Smith understood, would be crucial to the company moving from talented technologists to genuine movie-makers. The importance of story was one of John Lasseter's key contributions to the team, and one that differentiates Pixar from other companies. Not just providing strong storylines, but the ability to give the characters the illusion of life, to ensure that the storytelling worked.

> 'The subtle pantomime of believable dialogue, appealing drawings and most of all personal artistic statement may be beyond our reach in the mechanical area of electronic circuitry.'
>
> Frank Thomas, Disney senior animator, one of Walt Disney's 'nine old men'

John Lasseter respected and understood the principles of Disney's 'nine old men' – the core animation team brought together in the 1930s – but did not subscribe to their suspicion of computer animation. He worked on ways to release the comic and dramatic potential of his storytelling medium, to be even more nuanced and subtle, even more obsessive about detail than traditional animation.

He shared his mental model of what was possible and what was necessary with the rest of the team: 'The eyes more than anything else give life to a toy: the angle of a blink, how far the pupils go off to the side when a character is trying to peek at something without being noticed, conveys a sense of presence better than any other element.'

The dual obsession with story and great talent shaped Pixar's belief that the final decision rights should be held by the few best people in the firm. From a movie-making perspective the prime importance of a strong coherent story was reflected in John Lasseter having say over the final cut.

In technology and business terms the team believed that the same idea applied. Having seen Xerox fumble the future in terms of personal computing, and having been stymied by Sculley for the Macintosh launch, Steve Jobs was convinced that to achieve a universe-denting singular vision, many ideas are needed but in the end only the best should decide. It is testament to the strength of this conviction that, although he owned the majority of the company and felt an almost overwhelming need for control, Jobs empowered Catmull and Lasseter to deliver, as long as it was great.

Mapping the road to success

To translate their audacious vision into reality, the Pixar team agreed on a road map. It had three stages: producing commercials to help the animation team become self-supporting; making short TV specials to gain experience of larger scale production; and finally graduating to producing a full-length feature.

Later, in his triumphant return to Apple, Steve Jobs would deploy the same combination of focus and a strategy that linked radical breakthrough with relentless forward momentum. He stripped back the product line to the very few items that he felt could be game-changers. He laid out a phased plan to achieve dominance of the personal computing arena, from iMacs and iPods to iPhones and iPads, from iTunes to the App store.

Pixar produced their first commercial in 1989, for Tropicana, made five more in 1990 and another fifteen in 1991. Over the next few years Pixar would go on to make nearly forty more computer-animated commercials, the last being produced in 1996. They never moved on to the TV shorts stage, though, as on the back of *Tin Toy*'s success and Jobs' new-found vision, the strategy accelerated . . .

At Disney, a new management team of Michael Eisner and Jeffrey Katzenberg was looking to revitalize the firm. Disney had already become a major customer of Pixar, following Roy Disney's desire to automate the animation process using Pixar's Image Computers. Now they tried to tempt their alumnus John Lasseter back from Pixar. But Pixar's vision of changing the world proved too strong. Lasseter also recognized Jobs' loyalty over the last few years in defending the animation budgets while having to cut everything else at the loss-making firm.

Unable to persuade Lasseter to join them, Disney began to negotiate with Jobs about working together. In 1991 the team at Pixar negotiated a three-movie deal with Disney, the first of which would be *Toy Story*.

The shared vision of using technology and animation to tell compelling stories, and the road map for achieving it, united the team. It gave them common cause, helping them pull together and understand the different value that each of them brought to the table.

The legacy of Pixar's crucible moment

By 1993, with production for *Toy Story* in full flow, many of the ingredients of a great team were in place: a roster of the best talent from diverse backgrounds with distinctive skills, united in a shared quest and a common approach to pulling together. The team had been working together for years already. Many filmgoers thought *Toy Story* was an overnight success – in fact Pixar viewed it as 'the slowest overnight success in history'.

True high performance from the team only came into its own at the moment when the whole vision was endangered by the 'Black Friday' crisis triggered by screening the first cut of the movie. At the moment of everything going well, suddenly it seemed that everything was going terribly wrong.

Key creative Joe Ranft: 'We worked night and day and it was like the borders between us disappeared. We kind of melded into one. We were brutally honest with each other about what we thought wasn't working. And we evolved a way of working that I have never experienced anywhere else. We worked on each scene as a team. We became like one mind.'

Within that fortnight of hyper-intense activity, Pixar reshaped the opening third of the movie, placing their own stamp on it, changing character and story and trusting their own instincts and sensibilities. The Disney management team were impressed not only at the team's speed of response but also by how they had taken on board the spirit of the feedback.

Video graphics designer Ralph Guggenheim recalled, 'From the time we started through the darkest of times when production stopped and we feared the worst, we knew this was our sacred quest, we knew this was our holy grail and nothing was going to get in the way of getting it done.'

The shared intensity of facing a threat to everything they had worked for over the years bonded the team. The crisis, at a point where the team had nothing to lose, galvanized the formation of a superteam. It provided the catalyst needed to take all the existing ingredients and move them up to the next level. Ironically, the last-chance nature of the crisis removed the final barriers to the team becoming truly high-performing. Just like the experiences deliberately created during special forces training, the team was broken down to rebuild itself and emerge stronger.

Many great entrepreneurs, including Jobs and his equally iconoclastic friend Larry Ellison, founder of business software giant Oracle, have emerged from difficult childhoods. Nearly all great leaders have recovered from a dramatic career setback. Those are the moments when you discover who you are, what the best looks like in yourself. And that gives you the courage to go forward. The crisis gave Lasseter and the team the self-confidence and belief to follow their own ideas and instincts.

> 'You know what, let's just make the movie we want to make. We'll listen to their notes, but let's only take the ones we feel make the movie better and ignore the rest.'
>
> John Lasseter to the Pixar *Toy Story* team

Importantly, the *Toy Story* crisis forced the team to be more self-confident as individuals but also less ego-driven for the team. The team members put their own best ideas forward, not fearful of what others might say or think. Equally they were prepared to criticize and voice their concerns, trusting in each other to take the notes positively, focused solely on improving the film, literally looking at the bigger picture.

Through these testing times Pixar discovered an approach that enabled them to get the best from the diverse individual talents and play as a team, while not repeating the mistake they had made leading up to 'Black Friday' by trying to make a movie by committee.

In order to ensure the primacy of the story and maintain the compelling narrative that would distinguish *Toy Story*, Pixar's team made the clear distinction between encouraging everyone's full contribution and the final decision rights of the producer and director.

The crisis proved to be the tipping point for the creation of the team at Pixar. Perhaps if it had come any earlier in Pixar's development it would have broken the team. Instead, given the foundations of shared purpose, shared approaches and camaraderie, 'Black Friday' turned out to be a critical, positive moment of truth.

Looking back over the multiple blockbusters that followed, Ed Catmull and John Lasseter noted that the adversity they faced laid the foundations of Pixar's creative processes.

Specifically Pixar adopted two core processes. The Brain Trust brings the best of the best in the company into one room for a no-holds-barred discussion, at the behest of a director/producer team who have run into a problem. The director and producer have the right to refuse or ignore any comments and suggestions made by the Trust, freeing the discussion group to say exactly what they think and simultaneously liberating the director and producer from any sense of defensiveness.

Darla K. Anderson, who joined Pixar in 1993 after being inspired by Lasseter at a screening of *Tin Toy*, and went on to produce *A Bug's Life*, *Monster's Inc.* and *Toy Story 3*, says, 'The group is not for the faint hearted because telling each other the truth is a big part of being committed to each other's stories.'

The other core process is the Dailies: a meeting run every

day, attended by all members of the team, to review progress made. The notion of committing significant time to sharing work every day seems highly inefficient, constantly uprooting the plant to see how it is growing. The meeting, though, has a number of important objectives. First, it creates a climate where everyone can contribute and where the creatives do not feel the need to be too defensive about their work. Second, it ensures the director and producer can continuously steer the movie into a coherent whole.

Both processes seek to create the conditions experienced during the crisis that fostered the openness and trust which allowed the talented to express themselves freely and ensured the full contribution of the whole team.

'A movie contains literally tens of thousands of ideas,' says Ed Catmull. 'They're in the form of every sentence; in the performance of each line; in the design of characters, sets and backgrounds; in the locations of the camera; in the colours, the lighting, the pacing.

'The director and the other creative leaders of a production do not come up with all the ideas on their own; rather, every single member of the 200- to 250-person production group makes suggestions. The leaders sort through a mass of ideas to find the ones that fit into a coherent whole – that support the story.'

Jef Raskin, one of the leaders on the Macintosh team, observed that the perfectionist Steve Jobs 'would have made an excellent King of France'. Perhaps the truest test of the

Pixar team, and indeed Jobs' commitment to the integrity of the story, comes from the fact that Jobs never interfered with the creative process of the film-makers.

> 'We don't get a chance to do that many things and every one should be really excellent. Because this is our life. Life is brief and then you die, you know? We've chosen to do this with our lives. So it better be damn good. It better be worth it. And we think it is.'
>
> Steve Jobs

To infinity and beyond

Toy Story opened in 1995 to both critical and box office acclaim. It was the highest-grossing movie of the year, generating $192 million in US and $362 million in worldwide ticket sales. John Lasseter won a Special Achievement Oscar for his 'inspired leadership of the Pixar *Toy Story* team'. Ed Catmull, Thomas Porter and Tom Duff received the Scientific and Engineering Academy Award for Digital Image Compositing. The film was also nominated for best original musical score, best original song and best original screenplay.

As a breakthrough first feature, *Toy Story* was an incredible success. More incredibly, in the hit-and-miss movie world,

Pixar have remained virtually faultless in their productions. While future success is certainly never guaranteed, Pixar have been able to turn the creativity, conflict and cohesion required to produce *Toy Story* into a way of life that makes success much more likely. To date Pixar have produced twelve full-length feature films, winning twenty-six Academy Awards and grossing over $6.3 billion, using their proprietary RenderMan technology. The Pixar share flotation was bigger than that of the dot.com darling Netscape.

In 2006 Disney acquired Pixar for $7.4 billion. Steve Jobs became Disney's largest shareholder, owning 7 per cent of the company, and a member of the Disney board. When he died in 2011 Jobs' Disney shares were worth over $4 billion – twice the value of his Apple stock. John Lasseter became Chief Creative Officer of both Pixar and the Walt Disney Animation Studios, as well as the Principal Creative Adviser at Walt Disney Imagineering, which designs and builds the company's theme parks. Ed Catmull retained his position as President of Pixar, while also becoming President of Walt Disney Animation Studios. Most importantly for the team, they had touched the lives of the millions who watched their movies with magic.

> 'I believe in the nobility of entertaining people and I take great, great pride that people are willing to give me two or three hours of their busy lives.'
>
> John Lasseter

TEAM TALK Forging common purpose

At the heart of the Pixar story is the team's shared desire to make great movies using new computer technology. This is their common purpose. The starting point of any team is a challenge that requires collective action. No one individual could have created the technology, narrative and artistry that were fused together so successfully in *Toy Story*. Teams are the right answer to those missions and tasks which cannot be accomplished alone.

Pixar's success demonstrates the importance of a shared objective in attracting and combining diverse talents. The strength of the different skills and attitudes within Pixar is best epitomized by the mixture of three of its leading figures: the visionary Steve Jobs, the master of collective organizational structure and culture Ed Catmull, and the storytelling genius of John Lasseter. As with many others in Pixar, this triumvirate were leaders in their respective fields, with skills fundamental to achieving their shared goal. They all shared a desire to make magic through technology. Ultra-talented and driven, they also shared a history of bouncing back from setbacks, a resilience that perhaps gave them the added inner steel needed to pioneer an entirely new form of film-making. None of the three could have delivered the objective on their own. All three, working together, were necessary for success.

Great talent is a vital element of teams, indeed a necessity in the journey to superior results. But great individual talent also provides a significant challenge to great teamwork. Working with Steve Jobs has been described as unbelievable highs combined with unimaginable lows. The very elements that propel individuals to greatness, a certain narcissistic tendency, a forthright confidence, an ability and desire to take the initiative, can all lead to conflict within the team. The sparks that can fly when great individuals collide can ignite team performance or burn it to the ground.

Team chemistry and fit are also essential. Sculley and Jobs, regardless of initial enchantment, had no real meeting of minds. Nor did the similar personalities of Jobs and Alvy Ray Smith fare any better. However, there was enough cohesion and diversity between Jobs, Catmull and Lasseter for the team composition to work well. It was more than just common backgrounds and different skills. It was also fit in terms of personality and attitude towards power.

To harness this mix of high-calibre talent into superteam performance, Pixar concentrated on the shared objective. Making a 'great' movie was the overriding concern of each of the team. This common purpose enabled the team to evolve their approach to teamwork, and specifically creativity, solving problems and managing conflict. These aspects of teamwork came into sharp focus when Pixar faced their darkest hour during the *Toy Story* crisis.

> 'Pixar is made up of just a crazy combination of people. Thank goodness we found each other and created this familial tribe of people.'
>
> Darla K. Anderson, Pixar Producer

Unlike many of their competitors, Pixar also recognized the benefit of a stable core team. Rather than recruiting a new crew for each movie, Pixar focus on building a cohesive long-term team all committed to the same cause; to infinity and beyond a single movie.

Pixar believe strongly that in order to deliver the most creative ideas, everyone needs to be involved, and equally that in order to deliver a coherent compelling story the final decisions have to reside with the director and producer. The Dailies ensured all ideas were seen and heard, but only the best ones selected.

Pixar also discovered an approach that allowed them to have the right fights in the right way (essential, given the inevitability of intra-team conflict). The Brain Trust is an effective process for constructive criticism.

Both these approaches nurture the individual creative egos in the team and protect the delicate relationship bonds between team members. They allow strong personalities to disagree and not fall out without resorting to easy but weak compromises. These approaches were reinforced by courses focused on collaboration and teamwork in Pixar University. Most importantly, in defining a culture that blended a democracy of ideas and a dictatorship of decisions, Pixar maximized the chances of delivering a great movie.

A shared purpose inspires and binds a superteam to a common cause, an idea bigger than the biggest individual egos that come with the best individual talent. Whether in helping make decisions regarding team composition, the approach to collaboration or to overcome the many diversions, trials and tribulations, the common purpose served as a North Star, guiding the team forward on the long journey to *Toy Story*'s success.

Pixar's common purpose fulfils three fundamental characteristics that all teams can apply in improving their performance.

First, the objective itself required a collective response. No individual could successfully tackle the task single-handed. Making a movie meant inventing the technology, creating the characters, holding true to the narrative arc as well as funding it all. The goal required a team. Teamwork can often be the wrong answer to problems which would best be solved alone. Ensuring teams are deployed only where they are vital gives them a far greater chance of success.

Second, an effective common purpose needs to be clear and understood by the *whole* team. The definition of victory was unambiguous; making a feature film represented a clear finish line that the team could collectively aim for and measure progress against. Unlike some woolly visions, such as being a 'stakeholder champion', it was specific and measurable, leaving none of the team members in doubt as to whether they had achieved their goal or not. It was their equivalent of a Ryder Cup team's clear need to score 14½ points to secure victory.

The Pixar team collectively agreed on the destination as well as the journey to take. Developing a shared way forward requires teams to have a joint appreciation of their current reality. Steve Jobs needed to cut through his own reality distortion field to acknowledge that the firm had no future in being only a hardware or software company. Having faced up to their starting point and determined their destination, they connected the dots. The team at Pixar plotted a path from making adverts to television shorts leading to their ultimate goal of making movies.

A shared map should provide the team with milestones for the journey, rather than plotting every turn in the road. Too much detail will often be lost in translation as it is communicated through the team and will also be unlikely to allow for diversions in situation and circumstance, such as the Disney deal.

The test for shared clarity and understanding is simple. Can each member of the team articulate the same goal and the same path to achieving it? An effective common purpose means that when you shout 'Action!' everyone moves with the same clear direction.

Finally, Pixar's common purpose was compelling. The common purpose painted a vibrant and visceral picture of the future that the team found inspirational. Part of the inspiration came from the promise of arriving at their destination and part from the difficulty of the journey. The size of the task was highlighted in the technological breakthrough needed in moving from 500,000 to 80 million polygons. For the team at Pixar the stretch was motivating in the same way expeditions to unconquered territories are to explorers. Making a feature film was their 'putting a man on the moon' mission.

The road map was challenging but it was also feasible. Taken overall in one bite, the journey would seem impossible, but broken down into smaller chunks it seemed more manageable, still difficult but doable.

An important aspect of common purpose is that it tapped into the personal ambitions of each of the team members, giving their work real meaning. Rather than requiring individuals to compromise their own ideals for the team, the most effective team objectives are a broad church, harnessing team members' self-interests and their own personal motivations. Each of the team's members was personally driven by the marriage of innovative technology and the emotional power of art and storytelling. They had all pursued this ambition before Pixar and indeed would most likely have continued to do so even if they had not been members of the team.

Being a member of the Pixar team was compelling, as it provided its members with the best mechanism to fulfil their personal ambitions. As social animals, our own purpose often includes being a member of a team. To the best team players, belonging to a top team is motivating in and of itself and shared success is personally satisfying.

The research tends towards ranking shared commitment to the cause and challenge as a more important driver of team performance than shared commitment to each other. That is to say a common objective is more likely to deliver high performance than the relationship between members. The reality is that both matter and feed off each other – commitment to the challenge builds cohesion amongst the team. Cohesion between team members reinforces the commitment to the purpose. High-performing teams need both commitment to the cause and commitment to each other.

Like their spiritual godfather, Walt Disney, the Pixar team's objective was to 'make money to make movies, not movies to make money'. While the financial rewards from Pixar's achievements have been significant (for Steve Jobs they were even greater than his returns from Apple), they were a way of keeping score or a means to an end. There is no question that money and other external rewards can motivate people to commit and perform in teams, but the most powerful teams focus more on how those rewards will be earned, and connect with deeply held personal needs and motivations.

In addition to common purpose, the Pixar case also highlights the role that crisis can play. 'Black Friday' provided the added impetus to blend them successfully together. A crisis too early in a team's development runs the risk of crushing a team's confidence beyond repair. Yet without an urgent challenge the team may not make the final steps towards becoming a high-performing team. Moreover, surviving a crisis builds both individual and team pride and confidence, which in turn further fuels team performance.

Eyes on the prize, feet to the fire

Leaders and team members looking to turbocharge their teams need to establish a shared performance challenge that combines *both* the energy and hope embedded in an inspirational vision of the future *and* the sense of real urgency often associated with crisis. Performance challenges that meet both of these criteria are most likely to inspire the best individual and team performance as well as provide the strongest glue between team members.

As Steve Jobs commented, 'When I look back at my career

it's the things that were made under these circumstances, under the conditions that were not the best, that I am the most proud of.'

Pixar's success began with the idea of entertaining people, making them happy, through digitally animated movie magic. Not every team will have such audacious goals but all effective teams need to have a shared purpose that its members believe is worthwhile and stretches them beyond business as usual.

IIIIIIIIIIIIIIIIIIIIIIIIIIIIIIIIIIIIIIIIIIIIIIIIIIIIIIIIIIIIIIIIIIIIIIIIIIIIIIIIIIIIIIIIIIIIIIIIIIIIIIIIIIIIIIIIIIIIIIIIIIIIIIIIIIIIIIIIIIIIIIIIIIIII

AGENDA Forge common purpose

A clear and compelling common purpose is essential to attracting the right talent, inspiring them to want to do great work and to do it together.

Define the need for a team. Teams are at their best when they face challenges that cannot be mastered alone. An effective common purpose provides a clear and compelling reason for a team to exist. It is powerful in motivating the team to work together. The most basic and also the most profound question you need to answer is whether your challenge really needs a team. Unless your objective demands a collective response, you will get a poor return on the investment you need to make in building a team.

Make your common purpose compelling by making it personal and shared. While the poster may say there is 'no I in team', the truth is that the most powerful motivating force for attracting talent and unleashing high performance is often the most personal. The key is not to quash self-interest – since it is the most reliable and consistent human motivation – but to ensure it is aligned with the team's interest. Forging common purpose means discovering where interests are shared by individuals and the team and to enthusiastically reinforce, emphasize and engage those common interests. Focusing on 'the right thing for me is also the right thing for we' is a far more productive approach to building better teams.

Move hearts as well as minds. You need to inspire your team with a vivid picture of a better future. Aim to connect the team's work to an exciting, meaningful outcome, a result that is worthwhile to them. Often individuals and teams need to go beyond their current tasks and look at the ultimate benefit of their work and whom it helps. The volunteers in the Red Cross shops across Britain see their work selling second-hand clothes in terms of saving lives. They have a line of sight between their work and a cause that is bigger than any one of them. It may be indirect, but team members engage when they can see their contribution to the cause. Importantly, it doesn't have to mean anything to anyone else. It only needs to matter to your team.

Inject a sense of urgency. One of the most important tasks is to break through the torpor that can plague teams. Action will trump inertia when the alternative is worse. You need to turn your team's attention to the peril and the price of doing nothing. Make the most of a crisis and harness its focusing power to propel them into purposeful action. Build momentum through early successes which demonstrate progress is possible.

Go beyond business as usual. Shifting gears to become a higher performing team requires the energy and excitement of a real challenge. Embarking on an adventure where success is not guaranteed and is inherently risky will mobilize your team to do things differently. Becoming better will not happen by doing the same things in the same way.

Make sure your common purpose is clear and shared. It's little surprise that teams lose their way together when they can't agree where they are starting from and don't know where they are going, let alone how to get there. The simplest test of whether a team's purpose and goals are clear and understood by the whole team is to ask them. Getting each member to write down the team's objectives individually and then sharing them soon reveals whether the team is on the same page – or even on the same planet. Teams need a shared map: clarity on what success looks like, a realistic appraisal of their current situation and, based on these two points, to plot a path forward together.

Agree your definition of victory. Make sure your team has an unambiguous finish line to aim for. You need to specify simple goals and avoid complex or vague messages that can get lost in translation in a team game of Chinese whispers. If everyone shares the same specific understanding of what success looks like, when you shout 'Go!' everyone will move in the same direction towards the same target. For a sports team, the distinction between winning and losing is usually simple and clear-cut. The challenge for all teams is targeting the same level of clarity.

Take a robust view of your current reality. You need to take off your rose-tinted glasses – or in Steve Jobs' case, turn off the reality distortion field – and form a brutally honest assessment of what is working and what isn't. Taking the pain early enough to be able to do something about it is far better than the alternative of attempting to recover from failure when it is too late.

Chart the course together. Building the plan as a team will help you get the most out of your team. You can draw on the diversity of your team's experiences, expertise and perspective to build accuracy and robustness. In addition, involving the team engages them and fosters commitment to the purpose and plan.

Keep focused and keep flexible. Common purpose should remain a constant but the route taken will need to change in response to new events and fresh information. The analogy of sailing is helpful. Purpose is the North Star, the fixed point for navigating. The destination is set for each journey and the team needs to tack continuously to harness changing winds and make progress. You cannot fight the wind; you need to adapt and work with it.

Repeat, remind and reinforce often. Forging common purpose is a call to collective action. It should mobilize the team to get going together. Building momentum can require the most energy, but constant communication of purpose is required to maintain the pace over the bumps in the road and to stay the course in the face of seductive diversions. Forging common purpose is less about perfect wordsmithing or creating mouse mats with inspirational slogans that gather dust than it is about purpose being part of a vibrant and continuous conversation amongst team members.

'I didn't hit a shot out there. My players all played magnificently, all twelve of them.'

Colin Montgomerie

2
THE EUROPEAN RYDER CUP TEAM 2010
Captain and comrades

3.22 p.m., Monday, 4 October 2010, 17th green, Celtic Manor course, Wales

On the rain-delayed final day of the Ryder Cup, in the last and deciding singles match of the competition, Hunter Mahan misses a par-saving putt from just off the green and concedes the hole, and the match, to Graeme McDowell. With a handshake, McDowell, the recently crowned US Open champion, secures a wafer-thin 14½ to 13½ victory for Europe over the United States. The European captain, Colin Montgomerie, is in tears: he can't even watch the final putt, but the roar from the home crowd tells him everything he needs to know. Monty, dubbed 'Captain Fantastic' and 'Mr Montyvator', has not yet won a major himself, despite his talent, but finds sweet compensation by recapturing the Ryder Cup for Europe. Stung by criticism of his selection of Padraig Harrington as a wildcard pick, he'd said, 'Judge my choices after the Cup's over.' He and his team have triumphed in the most dramatic fashion.

A Ryder Cup team is an extraordinary team. Here is a group of very successful individuals who have been acclaimed – and handsomely rewarded – for their individual success, for their complete sporting selfishness. Tiger Woods happily says that winning in golf is all about dominating your opposition, putting your foot on the neck of your opponent and relentlessly pushing down until you succeed. Hardly the most promising material for a team.

After two years of mano-a-mano combat across the golf courses of the world, twenty-four of these super-individual talents are brought together for the biennial Ryder Cup competition, a team of twelve representing the USA against the twelve fielded by Europe. How do you take these inherently selfish people and mould an effective team ethos?

The key role is the captain's, again a quite remarkable role. The captain, like his players someone who has thrived on individual performance, since each captain has always been a world-class player, must – with no training, no track record as a leader, no rehearsal, no room for error – develop advanced leadership and team-building skills. Not only that, but the fruits of their team selection, coaching, tone-setting, motivation and tactics ripen in the full glare of the media and in front of 45,000 spectators and an estimated 650 million TV viewers, more than any other sporting event except the Olympics and the World Cup. That's pressure, to say the least.

Selecting the team to win

The starting point for the 2010 Ryder Cup teams was the selection of the twenty-four players who would represent Europe and America. Team selection for the Ryder Cup is a blend of automatic selection – based on form – and the captain's wildcard picks. The computer-ranked order of merit presented captains Colin Montgomerie and Corey Pavin with nine of their twelve players.

For his three wildcard choices Montgomerie trusted his own instincts. Here different factors came into play, not simply the players' skill level, but how well they would perform in the particular circumstances, one of the most pressured situations they might ever find themselves in, and how well they would function and perform as part of a team. This is where an intuitive understanding of human behaviour is essential. In 2006 captain Ian Woosnam selected Darren Clarke shortly after the death of Clarke's wife from cancer: some observers thought that Clarke would not be up for the challenge – he remained unbeaten in all his matches. In 2010 Padraig Harrington, Luke Donald and Edoardo Molinari were chosen over Paul Casey (at the time ranked world number 8) and the in-form Justin Rose.

Montgomerie says, 'My philosophy for selection for choosing three players out of the eight or nine who had a good case for being on the team had to go beyond pure golf. I had to consider how they would fit in with the nine automatic picks as friends, colleagues and partners, and how as teammates they would motivate the other players.'

Monty chose Padraig Harrington, despite a recent poor run of form, based on his past success in the majors and match play. 'Padraig has won three majors in the past two years,' said Montgomerie at the time. 'He has great stature in the game, and when his back is up against the wall he comes out and gives tremendous performances. He is someone we felt that nobody in match play golf wants to play.' Others, including the former winning US captain Paul Azinger, saw it differently, pointing to Harrington's lack of wins in the previous year and his poor Ryder Cup match history (one win from ten).

A number of potential team members for Montgomerie's European team had effectively *de*selected themselves by opting to play in a FedEx Cup tournament in Atlanta, a highly lucrative tournament but a non-ranking event for the European Tour. To Montgomerie and his vice-captains their decision pointed up a clear divide between Europe's golfing stars. Those who played in Europe in the less financially attractive but points-earning Johnnie Walker Championship at Gleneagles demonstrated that they wanted to be on the Ryder Cup team: for them the Cup and the team glory their selection represented was more important than cash, whereas the others showed less passion for the competition.

> 'I wanted passionate players who
> wanted to win for the European
> tour and not for themselves.'
>
> Colin Montgomerie

And in the end, with victory, it turned out that being part of a Ryder Cup-winning team might in fact prove better from an earnings standpoint because of the positive impact on players' individual brand image – self-interest and team needs coexist and even overlap to form common purpose. With his wildcards Montgomerie took the view that having players who were all motivated by playing for Europe, motivated by the same goal, would be more effective than better form. He made the decision that passion and fit with the rest of the team were the critical criteria.

On the US team Corey Pavin also faced criticism of his own wildcard choices. The inexperience of the young Rickie Fowler was questioned by some, whereas Pavin saw that the freshness and energy of youth would benefit the team. A lightning rod for fans and media commentators alike was the selection of Tiger Woods, chosen despite coming back from his much publicized off-course marital difficulties and fitness issues.

Tiger Woods is the greatest golfer, by wins, in the modern era and perhaps the greatest golfer of all time. By the time of the 2010 Ryder Cup he had won thirteen majors since turning pro. At his most dominant Woods played as if he was in a different league from his competitors. His twelve-shot victory at the US Masters in Augusta in 1997 underlined his super-iority. Woods had changed everything; he set new standards for the golf he played and the superstardom he attained. His sponsorship deals, $40 million with Nike and $20 million with Titleist, eclipsed any other previous deal in the sport.

It was in his mental game that Tiger's success was most striking. As with his hero Jack Nicklaus before him, Woods used his confidence like a weapon to cow his opponents. Woods learned mental toughness from a young age: his father Earl used techniques acquired from his own training as a Green Beret, a member of the US special forces, to condition his son. Tiger's mother Kultida was even more determined, part Chinese and part Thai and the personification, appropriately, of the Asian Tiger Mother. She pushed Tiger to stay focused on his studies and would confiscate his golf clubs until his school work was completed. She set high standards and was unafraid to make sure, often with physical reinforcement, that Tiger understood the consequences of any infractions. She also instilled in him his view of competition and in particular his killer instinct.

Kultida Woods taught her son that winning and competition meant stepping on the throats of opponents, fighting till the death and showing no mercy. 'That's sport. You have to. No matter how close friend you are, you must kill that person. When it is over, you can shake hand, be friend again.'

Tiger Woods is the product of his parents. He is super-focused and super-competitive, not just in golf but in everything. 'I love to compete. That's the essence of who I am.' Winning is not enough for him: it is important not just to win but to 'kick butt'. 'I want to be what I've always wanted to be: dominant. I'm aware if I'm playing at my best I'm tough to beat. And I enjoy that.'

After thirty years of deliberate practice, shaped from the most malleable time of his early childhood by his parents, and reinforced by continuous success, Woods is the ultimate individual golfer. Yet the very rituals, conditioning and fundamental approach to the game that drive success in the majors and other tournaments are hindrances when it comes to the Ryder Cup. Indeed many of the essential elements of Woods' armoury are designed to insulate him from everything else around him. Switching gears from being a killer on the course to being a supportive team player and – worse, perhaps – relying on others, is not just a rare occurrence, it is the opposite of the very approach that has been the secret of his success.

In Woods' five previous Ryder Cups this had been publicly evident. In 2002 he went out to practise on his own, earlier than his teammates, and he and his caddie were not always in team uniform. He had been on the losing side four times and on the winning team only once. Even in victory he rarely looked enthused or committed as a team member. His inclusion in the 2010 US team raised more questions about whether his presence as a team member would be an asset or a liability.

Montgomerie was well aware of the problem. 'Tiger is a tough person to partner with,' he observed. 'It puts real pressure on the playing partner to try and play up to Tiger. It's intimidating, and that's why his record in the foursomes and fourballs is poor for someone of his golfing ability.'

Creating the right environment

The blueprint Montgomerie relied on to construct Europe's victory owed much to Tony Jacklin, Europe's Ryder Cup captain from 1983 to 1989. Under Jacklin's captaincy the European team not only had their first victory in twenty-eight years, but triumphed for the first time ever in the United States when they won in 1987 at Muirfield Village, Ohio.

Until Tony Jacklin took charge there had been no real planning and no team infrastructure. Jacklin laid the foundations for a new approach to captaincy.

He focused on the course conditions: the captain and the home course greenkeepers can slant the advantage towards their own players, just as international cricket teams and groundsmen will tinker with their own pitches for each test.

Rather than create a level playing field (or perhaps more appropriately a level putting green) a European Ryder Cup captain will now typically shorten the course and narrow it at certain points to frustrate the big-hitting American team, alter the layout of the bunkers, adjust the height of the grass in the rough. 'I made sure there would be none of the fluffy long grass close to the greens that was the staple diet for Americans,' said Jacklin. 'I had all the areas round the greens shaved.'

Jacklin introduced uniform clothing for the European team (the Americans had initiated this some years earlier), co-ordinating the look to appeal to TV and boost morale by creating a team identity. He laid on a team plane, where previously each member had travelled separately, and invited the players' wives to be an integral part of the proceedings.

He set up a team atmosphere at the Belfry, the Warwickshire course where both Jacklin's home victories were achieved, with private rooms for dining and relaxation, and another where the players could get away from the hangers-on and generate a team spirit over days rather than trying to whip it up in a hasty huddle at the locker-room door.

He changed the format to suit Europe's lack of depth, increasing the number of fourballs and foursomes against the head-to-head singles. This insight would serve Monty particularly well in 2010. 'Tony took the Ryder Cup from three-star to five-star for the team,' he said. 'All the meticulous preparations we put into the uniforms, equipment and accommodation to make sure there were no distractions to the players were absolutely worth it.' Monty's strategy was two years in the planning. 'Everyone knew that the vice-captains and I had really thought about it.'

He did not change much of the course architecture, choosing only to slow the greens at Celtic Manor to dull the advantage of the Americans' putting. In a move reminiscent of football manager José Mourinho, he took over the microphone at press conferences to deflect attention from his players' difficulties and issues – Lee Westwood's torn calf muscle, Padraig Harrington's lack of form, Rory McIlroy's erratic putting. And he scored an early psychological victory when Corey Pavin managed to omit Steve Stricker from his team introductions.

Previous American teams had been buzzed up into a state of readiness by pep talks from golf pros who had served in the military. During the first Gulf War US captain David Stockton's 1991 team had turned up on the Kiawah Island course sporting camouflage caps. The US team had even drawn on President George Bush to instil a sense of patriotic 'backs against the wall' verve to the team, when he was invited in to rally a losing side with his reading of the Alamo Address. Previous captain Ben Crenshaw had added team shirts adorned with a photo montage of US winning teams to encourage a winning mindset.

There was some sense that this patriotic fervour could go too far. The 1999 Brookline tournament was notorious for its vocal and unpleasant atmosphere. Montgomerie was subjected to venomous abuse, Sergio García was called a 'spic' and García's US caddie Gerry Higginbotham was beaten up in a bar for being a turncoat. This chauvinistic aggression was not the spirit of the gentlemen's game, but saw the US victorious.

After the horrors of 9/11 and the postponed tournament in 2002 the spirit of the Ryder Cup returned with the realization that this was in fact sport and not war, and the fans were encouraged to be competitive but not corrosive. By 2010, there was some suspicion that Team USA had gone too far the other way when Corey Pavin's choice of lavender and baby blue team colours was derided by Fox Sports: 'Are they supposed to be warriors or interior decorators?'

In the rain that washed out much of the first day's play at Celtic Manor the US team's clothing proved worse than just unfashionable. Their waterproofs were not waterproof and neither were the team's golf bags, much to the annoyance of Woods and his teammates. Pavin ended up kitting out his men in standard-issue waterproofs hastily purchased in the club shop. Ian Poulter, speaking on behalf of the European team, was pleased to report that 'our waterproofs are working extremely well'.

Montgomerie had made trips to the Hong Kong golf-bag manufacturers specifically to ensure they were perfectly waterproof, and he applied the same level of detail elsewhere, providing extra-wide beds, for example, to guarantee a good night's sleep. Even the door to the locker room received attention: 'The door was solid and I was worried that someone could get hurt if it opened suddenly because no one could see who was standing on the other side. I replaced it with a door with glazed panels.'

Where Montgomerie injected his personal slant was in

introducing a sense of relaxation that was crucial in building these twelve players into a great team. He achieved it with an ease that belied his reputation as a dour, intense, sometimes tetchy player on the course, traits that led to him being dubbed 'Mrs Doubtfire' by his fellow pros.

Montgomerie set about creating an environment where the players wanted to play well, not just for themselves but for the team. Moreover, he knew players were motivated by being in the competition, but he needed them to feel relaxed enough to handle the pressure and to play to their potential. He organized quizzes during which light-heartedly blatant cheating was allowed, even encouraged, and arranged team dinners involving all the wives and girlfriends.

Football managers often say they want their players to go out and express themselves. Where Tony Jacklin had focused on self-belief, Montgomerie concentrated on creating a relaxed, comfortable and supportive environment that would allow the players both to perform at their best and to enjoy themselves.

Competing as part of a team adds pressure, either negative (you don't want to look bad in front of your peers) or positive (you raise your game for your teammates). Positive pressure is most likely to allow a player to express himself freely.

The job of the European captain is to take the twelve players from across the continent and forge them into a unit. The building of team spirit can never start too early: in his stint as captain Bernhard Langer was so hands-on and so keen to blend the mix of cultures into a team that he even developed a special meal for their flight to America. His main course fused British, Spanish, French and Irish ingredients while dessert was a traditional German Black Forest gateau based on his own mother's recipe.

Montgomerie sought help from the ailing Seve Ballesteros, battling cancer, as an inspiration for the team: Seve's portrait had pride of place in the team room all week. Ballesteros spoke to the team via a phone link – 'During the call to Seve, you could hear a pin drop,' remembers Montgomerie. 'The power of speaking to him was amazing. We wanted passion, and, by God, we got it from Seve.'

Graeme McDowell said his seminal Ryder Cup moment, even more than playing the winning hole, was on the Monday before the singles, seeing José María Olazábal crying in the team room in front of a photo of him and Seve playing together as partners in a previous Ryder Cup foursome.

The team room contained photographs of all of the players and their past moments of victory. Tellingly, Colin Montgomerie 'took down all the ones they had of me, because it was not me playing, but them'.

The team spirit in the European camp was palpable. They converted it into teamwork, supporting and inspiring each other. After a comment by Rory McIlroy that any member of the European team would want to play Tiger Woods in his current condition sparked a media frenzy, seven of his teammates all donned black wigs in tribute to McIlroy's trademark crop of black curly hair as they approached the first tee on the second practice day. Many kept their wigs on as they teed off.

> 'I don't want to let myself down this week.
> I don't want to let everyone else down
> this week. You're not playing for yourself.
> You're playing for eleven other guys.'
> Rory McIlroy

Team spirit was also in evidence when rain delayed play. The unexpected free time saw the Europeans relaxing together in the team room and in the treatment rooms. The Americans, meanwhile, fragmented, some retreating to their individual spaces to prepare in the way they would during an ordinary tournament.

Leading the team, developing leaders

Colin Montgomerie's personal support for the team members was paternalistic, in the tradition of Bernhard Langer, who knew just when to put his arm round a shoulder to give support and when to leave well alone. Monty was constantly telling his twelve players how good they were, rerunning highlights of their triumphs on DVD in the team room, cajoling anyone whose passion had dipped. His approach actively moved the team to a point where they could co-operate with genuine teamwork.

Equally, when he felt the players had failed to capitalize on the passion of the European supporters at Celtic Manor during the first day's play, on Day 2 Montgomerie was prepared to give them 'a bit of a bollocking – call it a pep talk'. Unable to address the team as a whole, given the succession of matches in play, he ensured each team member heard the same message: to make the most of home advantage and the 'thirteenth man'.

Different captains have different approaches, of course. Seve Ballesteros, a winner, acted like a benevolent dictator, becoming so caught up in the play that he advised his players on specific shots, often ones which only the genius of Seve would have been able to execute. The American Hal Sutton, a loser, used fear ('Every single player thinks Hal is about to bench them'). Montgomerie was the leader in the team room, firing up his men at the beginning and also in the meetings between each day's sessions. He was also the leader in choosing to step back and, as McIlroy says, enabling players 'on the golf course to go and do our own thing and let us play'. His experience as a player, and especially his unique Ryder Cup success record, provided the key to his ability to empathize with his players, show them respect and judge what they needed from him as their captain.

Monty took the courageous view, that non-playing vice-captains helped syndicate, not threaten, his authority. He knew that having additional pairs of eyes out on the course would noticeably strengthen his team. He could not be everywhere at once, and his vice-captains both guaranteed support for players wherever and whenever it was needed and fed back a constant flow of information. In addition to Darren Clarke, Paul McGinley, Thomas Bjørn and Sergio García, Montgomerie even persuaded José María Olazábal to become a fifth vice-captain on the second day when the format, revised due to the rain delays, meant there were six matches on the course at the same time.

It made a significant difference that his vice-captains had all been part of a winning Ryder Cup team in 2002. They already had a strong bond between them, a bond that facilitated the same spirit coming alive within the twelve players. Montgomerie also sought to involve all the players, trying to make sure everyone, including the rookies, felt equal.

Team spirit was of fundamental importance to victory. It created a situation where the players wanted to play for and with each other, and it enabled them to make the transition from twelve individuals to a single team. The evidence was on the course in the foursomes and fourballs. Fourballs are based on two pairs with each member of the pair playing their own ball and the best score from either side winning the hole. The key is for the first player in the pair to play the anchor role, hitting fairways and greens safely, giving their partner the chance to attack and take more risks going for the birdie. In foursomes, each player in the pair takes alternate shots, and the essence is to play for your partner, placing your shots where your partner wants the ball to be to play his best golf.

With rain washing out much of Friday, Montgomerie and

Pavin agreed a change in the format of the competition with the Cup referee. Both captains claimed to be pleased with the changes, agreeing that they represented the spirit of the competition. The changes meant that, for the first time in Ryder Cup history, all twenty-four players took part in six pairings at the same time. Ultimately, this arrangement better suited the Europeans since it increased the importance of real teamwork.

Team composition

> 'He was with every player and every player was with him. We didn't want to let him down. We wanted to deliver for Monty.'
>
> Padraig Harrington

In addition to his limited, though valuable, impact on the composition of the team, Monty had direct control over the choice and order of the pairings for the fourballs and foursomes and the order of the singles on the final day – whether to use his big guns to kick-start the session, secure the middle or anchor the rear.

Devising pairings was an area where previous captains had stumbled: notoriously the putting together of Woods and Mickelson by Hal Sutton in 2004 backfired badly. They were the number 1 and 2 players in the world, but the only bond they had was a mutual dislike. It was 'a partnership that made Tom and Jerry look compatible', wrote James Corrigan in the *Independent*. Even when Woods and Mickelson tried to relax in preparation for their pairing by playing each other at table tennis, their public attempt at ping-pong diplomacy only served to paper over the gaping cracks in their relationship.

Sure enough, Woods and Mickelson lost the first fourball of the 2004 Cup opening morning (to Montgomerie and Harrington), the United States lost that session by ½ to 3½ and the tone was set for an overall defeat. 'Langer was the second-best captain Europe could ever have wished for,' observed Monty. 'Sutton being the first.'

Paul Azinger, on the other hand, had persuaded the US tour to organize small match tournaments in the lead-up to the 2008 Ryder Cup so that he could see how individual players performed together. He made notes on who they said they would like to play with and, perhaps even more importantly, who they would *not* want to be teamed up with.

In line with his exacting preparation, Montgomerie had selected his starting pairs more than ten days before the match and had informed the players as well as the press. There were some natural pairings, as well as the opportunity to combine experience and the freshness of the rookies. For the first time the European side had two brothers – Edoardo and Francesco Molinari – whose close and comfortable relationship helped them combine well. 'I knew Francesco was quite shy,' remembers Montgomerie, 'and so when Edoardo came into contention it helped deliver a perfect partnership for the fourballs and the foursomes.'

The Northern Irish duo of McIlroy and McDowell were good friends as well as countrymen. 'They are friends but more importantly they respect and trust each other, and can rely on each other,' said Montgomerie. The pairings between rookie and experience also seemed to work well. Ross Fisher's play was inspired by his partner Padraig Harrington as they combined to beat Jim Furyk and Dustin Johnson on the seventeenth green. 'It was an honour to have a three-time major champion reading my putts,' said Fisher.

Montgomerie could not prepare in advance, however, for the decisions needed as the match unfolded with the rain forcing a change in format and the requirement for all twelve of his team to play in six pairings (as opposed to the usual four) at the same time. He did know that the fourballs and foursomes traditionally offered the best opportunity to convert team spirit into teamwork. He made a clear point of informing those two additional pairs who were now set to play that this new format really benefited the Europeans.

Such matches require players to go beyond cheering for each other to a level of collaboration and communication that is dramatically different from their normal individual game. Tunnel vision and a ruthless streak, which are both assets in individual competition, can become liabilities in the transition to teamwork.

Out on the course the Europeans' interaction went significantly beyond a show of high fives and fist bumps for great shots. Critically, the team left the word 'sorry' at the gates of Celtic Manor. Sharing a belief that they were all as committed as they could be, the team agreed that there would never be a moment where an apology for a shot would be required. This liberated the partnerships to play well for themselves and for each other; for the team and for the tour.

The Europeans led in all six matches at the beginning of play on Sunday. Montgomerie had ensured that the video display boards around the course broadcast the live scores, showing a board full of European Blue leaders and no US Reds, rather than the normal video footage. Montgomerie correctly thought that the scoreline would rouse the home supporters and the home team and dampen American spirits. By the end of the session, Europe had won 5½ points out of a possible 6, and were leading by three points, 9½ to 6½. Montgomerie's pairings and the teamwork on the course provided the engine of the Europeans' victory.

The choreography of playing order was never more serious than on the final day of the singles, with Europe needing to secure 5 additional points to regain the Ryder Cup. Montgomerie discussed the order with his vice-captains and determined that Lee Westwood should lead, followed by the real strength of Rory McIlroy, Luke Donald, Martin Kaymer and Ian Poulter to build on the momentum of the previous session.

Perhaps most importantly, Graeme McDowell was given

the anchorman slot, a position the recent US Open winner initially bristled at. 'My first reaction was actually to be a bit disappointed because I wanted to be in the mix when the Cup would be won, and I thought the other boys in the team would probably get the job done with me being a bit of a sideshow. Then I thought: "Wow, it could come down to me." And I felt excited.'

As the game reverted to a series of singles playing consecutively and in parallel, the US team began to claw their way back into contention. Steve Stricker beat Westwood in the first singles match, followed by further US victories for Dustin Johnson, Jeff Overton, Tiger Woods, Phil Mickelson and Zach Johnson. For the Europeans Ian Poulter and Miguel Angel Jiménez won critical games while rookie Rory McIlroy secured a vital half point. Luke Donald and Edoardo Molinari demonstrated the wisdom of their wildcards by winning a point and a half, respectively.

As the 2010 Ryder Cup came down to the very last match-up, Montgomerie's selection of McDowell as the anchor proved to be decisive. 'It was getting ugly out there, horrible,' said Montgomerie. 'It all changed the wrong way and it was left to Graeme, but he was put there for a very big reason.'

Even when the two teams were locked at 13½–13½ points with only the one match left, Montgomerie chose to ask Graeme McDowell, 'Do you want to know what's happened up ahead?' G-Mac responded that since Montgomerie had asked the question, he wanted the answer. Monty's analysis was simple. 'You have to win this game.' For McDowell, after the initial gulp of realization, the knowledge was critical in helping him refocus his mind, giving him clarity about what he needed to do. His shot on the sixteenth green, from fifteen feet, was 'the greatest putt of my life'. As they walked together up to the tee shot at the seventeenth Montgomerie played his final card as captain, offering McDowell critical advice and support. 'I had to remind Graeme there was so much adrenaline running through him at that moment, he must take account of it with his tee shot. That seven iron could go much further than he might have been thinking.'

'Somehow, having Colin there at that moment was a real comfort because I knew that he knew how I would be feeling,' said McDowell.

In the end the pressure took its toll on McDowell's opponent Hunter Mahan, who mishit his pitch to the green on the seventeenth. Europe had achieved the 14½ points needed to regain the Cup. As Montgomerie stated, everyone had confidence that Graeme McDowell, a proven champion under pressure, was the right man in the right place at the right time.

The change in gears for the players from individual gladiators to a fighting unit was challenging but the transition to leadership seemed to suit Montgomerie. As Padraig Harrington pointed out: 'I don't think his personality needs to change at all for being a captain. It's ideal in the sense that he does have the ability, as a captain should, to build up somebody's confidence or say a kind word to somebody. But I also believe that he has the ability to make the tough decisions that need to be made.'

Colin Montgomerie acknowledges that if he had performed as an individual in the same way that he had in the Ryder Cup, he would have enjoyed even more success. He is above all the ultimate team golfer, relishing the dynamic of relying on his teammates and even more importantly them relying on him. He won the 2010 Ryder Cup – with twelve players who in a straight match-up with their American counterparts were the inferior team, on paper – without playing a shot. He had created an environment where the team was meticulously set up for success, choreographing its members to maximize the benefits of collaboration, empowering leaders throughout the playing order and supporting his charges with vital personal coaching at the most critical moments.

This contrasts with the most successful golfer of the modern era, Tiger Woods, with his killer instinct and self-interested approach more narrowly focused on his own game than on others around him. Woods is indisputably a brilliant player, but how can a captain get the best out of him, beyond his own game, to serve the team? In this, Woods epitomizes the Ryder Cup team challenge, how to make a great individual a great team player. In the five tournaments that Woods competed before 2010, he won only ten points from a possible twenty-four. In the foursomes and fourballs he won six out of nineteen, losing twelve and halving one. In 2010 his record was Won 3, Lost 1 – perhaps chastened by the previous year's revelations, he was becoming more team-orientated. Maybe he is due a stint as a Ryder Cup captain – now that would be intriguing . . .

TEAM TALK Leading the team

At the core of the European Ryder Cup team success was the role of the captain. Like many team leaders, Montgomerie was 'promoted' into the role having proven himself as a team member. Indeed, as a team member Montgomerie has an unparalleled record of success in the Ryder Cup. As captain, however, he had to demonstrate mastery of a set of skills distinctly different from his own driving-and-putting game.

The first lesson that Montgomerie demonstrated is that the role of a team leader is very different from that of a team member. He could not lead by example as he had on the course; success had to come without hitting a ball. 'The one thing I had on my side,' he says, 'was the respect of the players. When it comes to the Ryder Cup I knew that I had their confidence *and* their respect because, without boasting, I had been there, seen it, done it, and won it.'

Too often team leaders, especially those who have been promoted based on their individual contribution – as best salesperson, best analyst or best programmer – fail to realize that the team leadership role is entirely different. New team leaders often fall into the trap of trying to achieve their team's objective single-handedly, acknowledging the greater challenge but seeking to meet it by working faster and harder as opposed to differently. More commonly, they try to make the team clones of themselves, attempting to ensure that every member acts exactly as the leader would (as Ballesteros did in selecting shots for his players that only he could make).

Montgomerie recognized his role as team captain was different from that of a team member. He left his clubs at home. His purpose was clear and compelling: bring back the Ryder Cup. His role as leader was defined, from the outset, by the 14½ points required to clinch victory. Montgomerie saw his leadership role as selecting the best twelve players, bringing the best out of each of them, creating the conditions for his team to win and, finally, turning a dozen professionally selfish individuals into a mutually supportive team.

Selecting the team

Team selection is in many respects the most critical decision any leader must make. That three-to-one split between form and instinct used by Europe in the Ryder Cup (the top nine players plus three wildcards) can work equally well in a business setting. The best talent for a team will typically be those people who are most skilled at what they do, who are most capable of fulfilling the task in hand. For the Ryder Cup team the main element of the task in hand is how well a player is hitting the golf ball and maintaining his nerve under pressure – those are the criteria. In a business context, if you are selecting a team member for a sales and marketing role, then you would choose the person who has been delivering the best numbers or building the best brand. Those team members will essentially select themselves.

Performance results often dictate the core composition of any team but diversity, attitude and chemistry amongst players also need to be considered. In picking Padraig Harrington, Edoardo Molinari and Luke Donald as his wild-cards, Montgomerie selected his 'best twelve' for the team rather than the 'twelve best'. He judged that their fit – with him, with the other nine players and under the particular pressures of the Ryder Cup – was of greater value than individual form.

The notion of fit and team chemistry also played an important role in the pairings of foursomes and fourballs. Based on the statistics of major victories, the combined strength of the world's number 1 and number 2 should be invincible. But as the Woods/Mickelson pairing demonstrated, the formula for team success is not linear and additive. Like too many chefs, a surplus of dominant characters can be unhelpful. The best partnerships will often benefit from complementary skills and attitudes. Montgomerie's own partnership with Bernhard Langer exemplified a successful partnership, the pair losing only one match in five Ryder Cups. Monty was known for speeding around the course whereas Langer was famously methodical and slow, and many observers felt Langer usefully tempered Monty's temptation to rush.

Montgomerie demonstrated that in defining the right team composition, team leaders need to consider both past performance and the chemistry between team members. In order to make these judgements team leaders need to know their team members well enough, in terms of skill and personality, to select and matchmake effectively.

Coaching for performance

Coaching team talent is often the critical difference in getting players to give their best. Monty translated his experience of being a player in the competition into becoming an effective coach.

Perhaps the most important lesson of his approach was to treat each of his team members as an individual. Pep Guardiola, when coach of FC Barcelona, said, 'Not all players are the same and should not be treated the same. You have to treat them with the same respect because they are people. But to bring the best out of them you have to treat them differently – to find the way to reach each one of them is what makes leading a team fascinating.'

Before the competition started Colin Montgomerie presented each team member with the gift of an oil portrait. Each portrait showed the player in team uniform standing by the same fireplace next to the Ryder Cup trophy. In portraying them all in the same layout and location the artist highlighted and captured the distinctive essence of each player. Monty had also developed a mental portrait of each of his team members, with real insight into their personality and their style, that enabled him to coach them most effectively.

Knowing your team that intimately is essential to being a capable coach. The best team leaders do not try to impose their own approach. Instead they help their team members find and enhance their own particular style of performing. Great coaches empower their teams to play their best game, which also tends to be their own game.

Rather than coaching the team with a 'one-size-fits-all' approach, team leaders do well by tailoring their coaching to each team member based on their individual needs. The best team leaders understand what makes their members tick and what specific type of support they need to succeed. While they all might benefit from being given a confidence boost, the best means of delivering one differs from individual to individual. For certain players it could be a pat on the back or a quiet word and for others public praise may be most potent.

The right time to coach is typically before, between and after performances, rarely during them. At the beginning it is about giving the team confidence. In the middle it is about getting them to consider what is working and what and how to change. At the end coaching focuses on asking the questions that enable the team member to learn and build on successes and failures. The rest of the time the coach's job is to get out of the way and allow the players to do their job.

Of course, there are exceptions to the rule. As Montgomerie demonstrated with his coaching of McDowell in the closing shots at Celtic Manor, the experience of having done the same tasks as your team members needs to be combined with knowing when to coach them. Choosing the ideal point to lean in and give the right support is the master's touch, often based on a veteran's empathy from a similar moment of truth.

An environment for success

Alongside selecting the right team and coaching the players, Montgomerie created an environment for success. Similar to English successes in the Rugby World Cup of 2003 and the Ashes in 2010–11, and British cycling's inexorable rise to world leadership following the 2004 Athens Olympics, Ryder Cup victory was built on a foundation of comprehensive and meticulous preparation. No detail was overlooked in creating the conditions for the team to be successful.

Team leaders ensure the team has the resources it needs to perform. Like other successful captains before him Montgomerie delivered the right uniforms, the right hotel accommodation and facilities for the caddies. He scrutinized the configuration of the scoreboards. David Brailsford, the Performance Director and mastermind behind British cycling, sees such meticulousness as 'the aggregation of marginal gains'. Ensuring that all the small, controllable things are done correctly sets the team up for success.

It is equally important to build the right culture. Montgomerie chose to blend passion with a relaxed, supportive camaraderie against the almost military firepower of the US team. The team events, the quizzes and the dinners, were conducted in an easy manner. Seve Ballesteros, especially given his ailing condition, delivered the passion. Monty sought to strengthen the sense of togetherness as a team by creating an atmosphere where the players felt comfortable with each other, where there was no need to apologize, where there was a strong sense of cohesion.

A significant element in creating a supportive team culture is how the leader acts. The team takes its cues from what the leader does. Team leaders are role models whose actions more than their words set the tone for how the team behaves. Montgomerie built his players' confidence rather than seeking to tell them what to do or critiquing their efforts. He sought their advice and consulted them. He treated them as partners.

The right culture is more than team *spirit* and good morale, it focuses on actual teamwork and on supporting each other to win matches. The wig-wearing support given to McIlroy was both fun and a demonstration of teamwork – the active support of team members for each other. Montgomerie encouraged and celebrated such displays of support, effectively rewarding and reinforcing teamwork as the right behaviour.

Teamwork was crucial in the fourball and foursomes, where support and collaboration between the pairs became the engine of Europe's victory.

A team of leaders

In choosing and empowering his large team of vice-captains Montgomerie also demonstrated an important lesson in team leadership. He ensured that the job of supporting team members, of creating the right team spirit and encouraging teamwork, was not his alone, but a shared responsibility across the team. He was the catalyst and architect for the team, but he recognized that the team would be more powerful if he did not have a monopoly over its leadership.

Montgomerie understood that, in the ideal team, all members would act as team leaders; they would all support, coach and inspire each other. In that sense the culture that Monty was promoting was one where team leadership became a task for all team members, not just for him.

At the beginning of a team's existence the team leader's role is as first amongst equals. The leader has the primary role in defining the composition and coaching the players for peak performance. The team captain is also the architect of success, creating the conditions and delivering the resources the team needs to win. But as the team develops, so team leaders need to create a culture where all team members play a team leadership role. Real success is when a team leader transforms a constellation of individual stars into a stellar team.

||||||||||||||||||||||||||||||||||||||||||||||||||||||||||||||||||||||||||||||||||||||||||||||||||||||||||||||||||||||||||||||||||

AGENDA Lead the team

All teams need leadership and the best teams are well led. Leadership in teams is a distinct but equally important task to deliver better results. The starting point is a formal team leader. The goal is a team of leaders.

Team leadership is its own task. Leadership in teams covers three core responsibilities. You are responsible for (1) delivering the team's objectives, (2) building a cohesive and effective team and (3) managing and developing individual team member performance. The three are separate but related. Helping individuals become better team members is essential to building a better team, which in turn increases the chances of achieving your team goals. As a team leader you need to juggle these three balls, and not drop any of them – in addition to any task responsibilities you may have as a member of the team.

Leadership means going first and last. As the team's leader you are the architect of the team. You start with primary responsibility for all of the tasks of building and managing your team to deliver results. As well as going first you also remain fully and finally accountable for whether your team wins or loses: the buck stops with you.

Leaders flex their style. Rather than having a preferred or dominant style, you need to be able to shift the way you lead between the four core styles of leadership to suit the situation and the individuals on the team: *Controlling*, *Coaching*, *Consulting* and *Collaborating*.

Controlling. At the beginning of a team's life or your tenure as the team leader, when you do not yet have the insight into the team's capabilities, the right approach is to exert authority and control. It is easier to start tight and loosen control as needed. A firm hand on the tiller is also needed when fast decisions are required or when team members have reached an impasse, especially where you have significantly more and better insight into what to do. In these situations specific clear instructions and close supervision are appropriate. Your focus is on giving your team what they need to be able to fulfil your common purpose.

Coaching. Where team members are more skilled, your role as leader needs to shift to guiding the team, giving critical advice at key moments. Building confidence with team members is the central focus in preparing the team before its performance challenge. This is less about vacuous exhortations of 'Go team!' than it is about reinforcing the team's belief in its potency. Specific reminders of actual individual and team past performance, when they were performing at their best, helps put the team in the right state of mind. While you are coaching your whole team, you should not forget that you are first and foremost coaching people. Tailor your approach to each individual and their particular needs; find an approach that works for them.

Consulting. Have the confidence to recognize where you might not have the right answer. If you believe that the team may know best, your focus is to invite discussion and ask the right questions. What worked well, what needs to change, how will we do that? Your role is in helping your team discover their own insights, encouraging them to own their own performance and learn from it. You are looking to support them in taking greater responsibility for future action. Developing individual members is an important means of developing your team, and growing your team's capabilities is one of the best ways of improving performance.

Collaborating. When the team is in full flight and performing effectively, effective team leaders know when to get out of the way. This is what you are aiming for and building towards: the moment when you can hand over the remote control to the team. By shifting through the gears from control to coaching and consulting, your role is to build the team's ability to take over the tasks of leadership. In this style of leadership, you will increasingly be collaborating as a first amongst equals in a web of mutual accountability.

Create a team of leaders. Your team will perform at the highest levels when individual members also take up the mantle of leadership, when they share your capability and commitment to build a better team. Developing leaders across the team is developing a better team. The strongest teams are those where more members inspire, support, challenge and hold each other accountable. Yet even in teams full of capable leaders there will still be situations, such as facing crisis or great change, where you will need to switch your style. After all, you remain accountable. In that sense a leader's work is never done.

'"Who dares wins" is a way of life. It is living and breathing this motto that makes the SAS the best at what they do.'

Andy McNab

3

THE SAS
IRANIAN EMBASSY
SIEGE TEAM
Camaraderie and clarity

1924 hours, Monday, 5 May 1980,
the Iranian embassy, Prince's Gate, London

Five days after terrorists supporting the independence of Iran's Khuzestan province have taken twenty-six people hostage at the Iranian embassy in London, the situation comes to a head. Over a Bank Holiday weekend the tense stand-off between the terrorists and negotiators representing the UK authorities has been played out in the full glare of media scrutiny. During the course of the weekend five of the hostages have been released, but on the sixth day one of the remaining hostages is murdered. Immediate action is vital to save the others. There is now no way back. The decision is taken: send in the SAS. At 1907 hours on Bank Holiday Monday the SAS teams surrounding the Iranian embassy receive the order to attack. Seven minutes later the codeword 'Road Accident' informs them that a key explosive distraction device is now in

place. Nine more minutes, and a second codeword, 'Bank Robbery',
indicates that a unit of SAS soldiers is ready to abseil down from
the roof. And one minute after that, the one unmistakable order:
'Go! Go! Go!'

From start to finish the operation to relieve the siege lasted seventeen minutes. By the time it was over five of the six gunmen had been killed, the sixth safely captured. Only one of the remaining hostages died in the course of the rescue. Just over a quarter of an hour of intensive action bore all the hallmarks of the SAS: a daring raid based on meticulous planning and preparation, combined with improvisation under fire, individual acts of bravery and seamless teamwork. And the team that carried out the attack – watched by millions live on TV – proved the value of the SAS's commitment to the core principles of team composition, team selection and training.

The SAS blueprint for action was, and remains, based on principles that date back to the regiment's inception during the Second World War and its years of special forces experience throughout the remainder of that war, and later during the Malaya Emergency of the 1950s and in Oman in the 1970s.

The SAS came into being in 1941, during the North Africa campaign. David Stirling, a Scots Guard, had previously been recruited as a member of the new 'Commando' brigade, a guerrilla force which had been devised by Winston Churchill to operate, as he put it, like a 'pack of hounds' and a 'band of brothers'.

Churchill's vision was of a new kind of egalitarian fighting force within which officers and non-commissioned men would work alongside each other in an atmosphere of self-reliance and individualism. The Commandos would provide the kind of flexibility and fleet-of-foot response that could match the enemy's ultra-modern military technology, the kind of flexibility which had been singularly lacking in the lead-up to the evacuation from Dunkirk.

Stirling, who enjoyed both his drink and his gambling, had been described by the Guards assessors as 'irresponsible and unremarkable'. The assessment of the 8th Army's commander, General Bernard Montgomery, is perhaps more telling: 'He's mad, he's quite mad,' he once said. 'But in war we need people like him.'

After being badly injured during a practice parachute drop, Stirling heard that the Commando force was about to be broken up. On crutches but still adeptly managing to avoid security, he made his way into the office of the Deputy Chief of General Staff and handed in a proposal for 'the retention of a limited number of special service troops, for employment as parachutists'. This was the starting point for the Special Air Service.

That the SAS ever saw active service was down to the combination of Stirling's maverick, anti-Establishment approach blended with two other ingredients provided by key colleagues.

Jock Lewes, an Australian Commando officer, added an add-itional level of detail, intense analysis and the nuts and bolts to Stirling's broad initial structure. Paddy Mayne, a former boxer and British Lions lock forward, brought physical excel-lence and the warrior spirit into the mix. Combined with a shared sense of self-deprecating humour and humility – an attitude which later protected the SAS against accusations of bragging, and hence resentment from other regiments – this was a potent cocktail, and a mix of characteristics that has underpinned the profile of the ideal SAS soldier ever since.

Selection: the quest for the best

The SAS selection process is designed to identify the core characteristics of that ideal soldier through a series of often brutal (and very occasionally lethal) tests. The SAS only ac-cept volunteers from existing members of the armed forces and the part-time territorial SAS regiments. Even to war-hardened professionals from the Parachute Regiment, the SAS selection procedure is known to be the toughest of any military unit in the world.

Lasting six months, selection training is broadly divided into three core phases. The first focuses on fitness and naviga-tion, the second phase centres around jungle training and the third on combat and survival. Each of these phases is designed to pick out those soldiers who have the requisite but rare mix of physical endurance, mental toughness and unorthodox intelligence demanded by David Stirling's original conception of the unit.

The first phase takes place during a month based in the hills of the Brecon Beacons in Wales, culminating in Test Week and the endurance Long Drag. The first three weeks are designed to build up recruits' fitness and stamina through continuous cross-country marches, known as 'tabs', which start at 0400 hours and end long and late into the night. Candidates have little time to rest and recover, even as the pace and the demands increase relentlessly.

Time limits require the candidates to jog for much of the distance, over rough and steep terrain. The weight of the loads in their backpacks is increased to 25kg, with the straps cutting painfully into deepening sores on tired shoulders. The tabs demand relatively simple navigation across flattish terrain and are carried out in groups of four, but then evolve into uphill navigation at night in pairs, followed by even longer tabs carried out as solo missions, testing individual capabilities throughout the day and night.

The high level of physical exertion opens up potential recruits to real mental pressure. Given little direction beyond a rendezvous point and the only instruction being to get there 'as quickly as possible' serves to add uncertainty, especially to those soldiers more used to the detailed and prescriptive nature of other military units. Deprived of sleep and physically stretched, the 'superfit' candidates frequently drop out during the gruelling endurance elements, because they have never been in a position of utter exhaustion before. Sheer brawn alone is not enough. Unshakeable resolve, inner determination and self-belief are more important than physical prowess.

By the time Test Week arrives many candidates have already departed by choice, unable to commit to the demands of the process. Others will have been 'binned', deemed unsuitable for the challenges of the three weeks of relentless physical tests. Returned to their units and regardless of how well they may have performed up to that point, their photographs are stuck up on the wall of the HQ and given the SAS's own brand of plastic surgery with a stark red line scrawled across them.

> 'Test Week was indeed a bastard.'
>
> Mike Curtis, SAS veteran

After the final endurance challenge of the Long Drag, a time-limited forty-mile night-time tab including the monster hill of Pen y Fan, typically less than 30 per cent of the recruits are left. For those who do make it through Test Week, far harder tests await, provided by five weeks of jungle training in Brunei or Belize. During this phase of selection, recruits are tested and trained in parallel. Standard Operating Procedures, SOPs, especially those based on strong teamwork such as fire and manoeuvre, are taught and continuously drilled into four-man teams until they become second nature.

Discipline, a core tenet of the SAS, is again at the fore-front. Learning and executing new drills with live rounds is made even more challenging after three weeks of being per-manently soaked to the skin, covered in festering cuts and leeches. The final exercise – to locate and attack an enemy base – is designed to test precisely how much of the jungle training has been absorbed and requires the team to navigate and avoid detection for eight days. The team must commu-nicate in silence via Morse code and signals, living on 'hard routine': water and cold rations with no naked flames permit-ted for cooking. As one graduate, Mike Curtis, remembers, 'We had to shit into a plastic bag and take the whole lot with us, leaving no trace of our existence behind.'

Once again, the number of recruits who make it through this phase is less than 30 per cent of those who started it. The final stage of selection training is combat and survival, focus-ing on escaping and evading detection. This stage culminates in a survival exercise which is followed by a twenty-four-hour interrogation combining physical punishment, sensory deprivation and psychological torture.

'I couldn't believe this was only training,' recalled Paul Bruce. 'I knew the SAS was tough and the training rigorous but this seemed beyond credibility ... It was not knowing where or when I would be hit next that upset me. I lost track of time; I lost track of what to say to try and put an end to this bloody agony.'

The difference between those who wilt during the toughest

phases of selection and those who go on to earn their SAS badge is the ability, even when the body is screaming for sleep or an end to pain, to apply rigid mental discipline, the preparedness to keep going, to complete the mission. Those few with the mental toughness not to break are finally deemed worthy of wearing the famed winged dagger badge of the regiment.

> 'I didn't have to travel 300 kilometres on foot with no food or water during selection, but I did display the mental fortitude and discipline which prepared me for Iraq.'
>
> Chris Ryan, member of Bravo Two Zero patrol

The fearsome reputation of the process means that only those few who believe they have the potential will apply, and the fearsome practicalities of it mean that nine out of ten will fail. There is no standard or obvious SAS type. Certainly class, race and background have never played any role in selection. Excellence in attitude and ability has always been far more important than background. Selection is a rigorous and purposefully elitist process designed to eliminate all soldiers except the few that fulfil the SAS's specific definition of excellence. Or as Lofty Wiseman, a former SAS member, puts it, 'Death is nature's way of telling you that you've failed selection.'

This ruthless filtering process ensures that the regiment

has the best available talent for the most extreme arm of the British military. Moreover it cements the self-belief essential in every member of the SAS. They trust in their own abilities to deliver.

'Selection is designed rather to find an individualist with a sense of self-discipline than the man who is primarily a good member of the team,' says Major Clarence 'Dare' Newell, 'for the disciplined individualist will always fit well into a team when teamwork is required, but a man selected for teamwork is by no means always suitable for work outside the team.'

This individual test is – almost paradoxically – an important foundation of teamwork. Every member of the SAS is aware that their teammates have also passed the trial by fire. Knowing that everyone else in the regiment is also made of the right stuff ensures that, even in the fog of war and when it matters most in instances of life and death, they can rely completely on the capability and commitment of their colleagues.

The selection process has proved so successful that it has been adopted in various guises throughout the world. The US Army Special Forces' assessment and selection programme's slogan is that 'your mind is your best weapon', reflecting the emphasis the SAS selection places on mental toughness. US Navy SEALs – whose Iranian embassy moment was the killing of Osama Bin Laden in his compound in Abbottabad in May 2011 – have also built on the SAS focus, 'training the best and discarding the rest'.

The SEALs take the precept of making training as close to real combat conditions as possible to the extreme. Within days of joining the selection process, candidates undergo an exercise – or an 'evolution' as the SEALs instructors call it – which is called 'drown-proofing', essentially having your hands bound behind your back, your feet tied together and having to swim underwater. It is like volunteering for a dose of waterboarding.

While the SAS focuses primarily on testing the individual, the raw material of teamwork, passing selection is a shared rite of passage. It creates a common experience between individual members of the SAS that unites them as a band of brothers, just as Churchill had imagined.

The selection and training programme for each SAS soldier is, in the words of David Stirling, 'an exhaustive one designed to give him thorough self-confidence and just as importantly equal confidence in his fellow soldiers' capacity to outclass and outwit the enemy by use of SAS operational techniques'.

The rigour of selection allows recruits to prove their individual capability both to themselves and to each other. Together, this trust in self and trust in each other provides an essential basis for strong teamwork.

For the team of SAS troopers preparing for the assault on the Iranian embassy, the knowledge that they had all passed selection training provided a quiet confidence in the skill and the will of each of the men around them.

Structure and detail

When the terrorists first burst into the Iranian embassy on 30 April 1980, and as soon as the scale and severity of the attack became obvious, army chiefs activated the special forces. A four-digit code – 9999 – was sent by pager to the Special Projects or SP team, the SAS's anti-terrorist unit available on a round-the-clock basis for immediate response in mainland Britain.

The responsibility for handling anti-terrorist operations rotates between the four SAS fighting divisions, Sabre A, B, D and G, every six months, ensuring all divisions develop expertise in hostage and terrorist situations. As with everything related to the SAS, the structure is designed to serve the mission and achieve operational objectives.

The four Sabre divisions are further structured into four sixteen-man troops, each specializing in a different 'insertion skill'. Air Troop train for parachute-based missions, Boat Troop have an expertise in above- and below-the-surface amphibious missions, Mountain Troop are trained and practised in climbing, skiing and winter warfare, while Mobility Troop focus on transportation of all kinds.

Form also follows function in the SAS's basic four-man operating unit. From its earliest missions infiltrating deep into enemy lines in North Africa to destroy German planes on the ground, the SAS has relied on the four-man team as the optimal size for ease of movement, concealment and the 'total exploitation of surprise and guile' central to their task.

The balance of individualism and teamwork observed in selection training can also be seen in the specialization of the squad members. A careful record is kept of each soldier's particular aptitude in the various skills: weapons, communications, engineering, medicine, languages, intelligence and sniper accuracy. This register of special skills is vital to ensure that each team contains the right blend and balance of skills and characteristics needed to complete its mission.

But given the need to complete the mission, even if team members are captured, injured or killed, each member also needs sufficient ability across all of those areas to be able to take on any of the other roles at a moment's notice. Each team member also has the task of training other team members in their chosen field. This shared responsibility reinforces the need for individual expertise to be maintained and skills to be further honed. The team exerts a professional pressure on each member to be the very best they can be.

Working, training and living closely together, often in adversity, creates an almost telepathic understanding between the four team members. The small size of the unit, and indeed the small, elite and secretive nature of the SAS, also contributes to the formation of tight bonds between team members and the strong levels of cohesion in the group. They say that it is all right for an SAS soldier to take a comrade's girlfriend but *never* their ammo.

In addition, the small-unit cohesion is increased through the SAS's distinctively egalitarian culture, with all ranks in the SAS being of 'one company'. In line with the drive for excellence, experience is often seen as more important than rank and so overall command may be given to a sergeant rather than an officer who has less experience. The sense of team is also reinforced through 'Chinese Parliaments': planning meetings, often held during live operations, where the views of all team members are given equal consideration, irrespective of rank.

Preparation and planning

As the SAS team members gathered at the main HQ, Bradbury Lines in Hereford, they were hopeful that they *would* be required for action, since this was the kind of operation they spent their days training for but rarely encountered. As one observer commented, 'They felt they trained and trained – but you could only sharpen a knife so much. What they wanted to use was the edge.'

For four days the SAS carried out non-stop planning and practice, not knowing when or whether the order would come. Accurate and timely intelligence of the situation in the embassy was vital. The advance command group – the 'head shed' in special forces parlance – had quickly set up a main base station or MBS at Regent's Park Barracks, a mile or two from the Iranian embassy. The imminent action was code-named Operation Nimrod. While the MBS awaited the arrival of the SAS squads and started reconnaissance and planning, the Metropolitan Police began the standard protocol of 'ICC' – Isolating the incident, Cordoning off the perimeter, and Containing and negotiating the crisis.

The Met's own command group set up camp in the Royal Needlework School, close by the embassy, but then had to move on because their constant smoking was jeopardizing the school's precious tapestries. They relocated to the Montessori School next door, where they were given permission to remain only so long as they promised to feed Mr Nibbles, the school gerbil.

To mask the noise of drilling as surveillance cameras were threaded into the embassy, fictitious gas leaks were created in the surrounding roads so that pneumatic drills could cover the sound. Flight paths of commercial jets from Heathrow were diverted overhead to add further distraction.

The SAS – in two teams, Red and Blue – arrived at the Regent's Park Barracks at 0300 hours on Thursday 1 May, and received a detailed briefing, known as 'green-slime', from Military Intelligence. Each SAS member made individual intelligence boards, including details of the hostage-takers' movements, noting that PC Trevor Lock, one of the hostages, was still armed, and learning and memorizing the faces of both the hostages and hostage-takers.

An initial crude plan, effectively a 'bloody' frontal assault, was quickly developed to deal with the need for immediate action. In parallel Red Team were deployed in civilian dress to reconnoitre the embassy and gather more insight to form a plan which would have higher chances of success. Based on the intelligence gathered, Lt Col Rose and Major Gullan of the SAS developed a detailed Deliberate Assault Plan.

Like all SAS operations, the mission objective was kept ruthlessly simple: to rescue the hostages inside the building. No more, no less. Everything the soldiers would do, if and when they had to assault the embassy, would be focused on that one objective, all decisions informed by it. To ensure there was absolutely no doubt, the mission was confirmed twice in the formal operational orders given by Director SAS Brigadier Peter de la Billière.

Unspoken but no less clear to the SAS was Prime Minister Margaret Thatcher's direction that she did not want any ongoing problem. 'We were fairly certain that they didn't want any martyrs ... no surviving terrorists,' recalled an anonymous SAS trooper.

The Deliberate Assault Plan itself was broken down into five clear phases: deployment; initiation and entry; stronghold assault and domination; evacuation; and post-assault. Each phase had a clear definition of what success was, and operational elements detailing the roles and responsibilities of the various teams so that each of the fifty-five soldiers, divided into eight units, moved in seamless co-ordination.

'God is in the detail' is an SAS mantra. Each team knew

precisely how they would enter every room, who would go in and in what order, who would cover the others, how the room would be cleared and explicit 'limits of exploitation'. Having cleared and secured their designated area the teams would stop and consolidate, only continuing if needed to support another team. The preparation balanced the mission objectives and the need to avoid the nightmare of a 'blue on blue', the shooting of a colleague in error.

Part of SAS standard training is the use of the Killing House, a purpose-built facility with rubber-coated movable partitions designed to soak up live rounds and to enable reconfiguration into different layouts. The Killing House is used by the SAS for close-quarter combat training, relentlessly practising the speed and teamwork necessary for mission success. In preparation for the potential assault on the Iranian embassy, the Irish Guards' Pioneers had constructed a physical mock-up of the rooms in the embassy that was as realistic as possible. This allowed the SAS to rehearse every move, so that each four-man team could operate as a unit, as 'a single animal'.

A full alternative plan to the stronghold assault of the embassy was also being developed, focusing on the scenario of rescuing hostages from a bus transferring them from the embassy towards Heathrow (which was one of the hostage-takers' demands) and requiring the teams to spend time training for the rescue using a forty-seater bus in a large garage at Regent's Park Barracks.

Even during the mission itself the SAS continued to

rehearse and run mental drills in preparation. Lance Corporal John McAleese, responsible for blowing out the entrance to the front balcony, was visualizing how he would place the frame charges on the window right up until the moment the 'Go!' command was given.

'In life-and-death situations, fear can cause men to freeze – totally immobilize them,' says Dick Couch, a former SEAL officer. 'Often only the confidence instilled by repetition and drill can get them moving.'

The thoroughness and simplicity of the plan ensured that every soldier knew his role, understood how it fitted with the objectives of his own team and understood clearly how it would synchronize with the other teams. The constant training and rehearsal gave them the confidence that they could execute the plan with the necessary speed, aggression and surprise.

Flex within the flux

Experience, however, had taught the SAS that no matter how well-planned and rehearsed a mission, the most unexpected things could go wrong. No plan survives first contact with the enemy, or in more prosaic SAS language 'there is always the fuck factor'. They had learned, often the hard way, that things might always get worse. Central to the SAS ethos was to prepare thoroughly, with contingencies and 'What ifs?' systematically explored. Of equal importance was to build in

operational flexibility, to select and train for the improvisation and individual decision-making necessary to react to the
situation as it was unfolding.

Unlike the terrorists, who by comparison were somewhat
ramshackle, the SAS soldiers knew how to move as a highly
co-ordinated unit. Success was based on their well-honed
individual capabilities and the freedom to operate within the
rehearsed framework of the assault plan, all governed by the
overriding objective of rescuing the hostages.

The preparedness to react and improvise has been a feature of the SAS since raids in the Second World War saw
soldiers disabling enemy aircraft by hand when they had run
out of explosives. It was critical in overcoming the inevitable
unexpected factors at Prince's Gate. The sound of one of the
team breaking a window as he moved into position alerted the
hostage-takers and Major Gullan made the instant decision
to jump from deployment to insertion. Hence, instead of the
planned command of 'Standby, standby', he went straight to
'Go, go, go . . .'

'"Go, go, go! Get in at the rear!" the voice was screaming in
my ear. The eight call signs rose to their feet as one and then
we were sweeping in through the splintered door,' remembered Trooper Pete Winner.

More hiccups immediately ensued. Two of the abseilers
of Red Team became snagged in their ropes. The embassy
curtains, which the gunmen had soaked in petrol, caught fire
from the stun grenades the SAS had used, again not to plan.

The hostage-takers set alight the barricades they had built, blocking the way to the room where hostages were held. Soon the spreading fire became as much of an enemy as the six armed terrorists.

Overcoming these challenges necessitated great individual courage, quick thinking and decisive action. Lance Corporal Tommy Palmer's scalp was 'crisp to the touch' after he was forced to take an unplanned route through burning windows to access the building. Red Leader had suffered second-degree burns on his legs from the fire that engulfed him as he hung jammed on his abseil and he completed the mission despite fierce pain.

In many respects the chaos suited the better trained SAS. Indeed they had created some of it themselves. Detonating a large explosive charge lowered into the atrium caused panic and confusion, providing the surprise element the SAS needed to distract the terrorists and to allow them to enter.

With the phase-three 'assault' element underway, but 'domination' not yet achieved, phase-four 'evacuation' was taking place in parallel, the sections of the Deliberate Assault Plan overlapping like the flames from the growing blaze. Through the thick smoke and the cacophony of wall-shuddering explosions, staccato bursts of machine-gun fire and terrified screams, the rescue of the hostages remained the clear imperative for the SAS.

'We were throwing them like rugby balls, person to person down the stairs,' said team member Robin Horsfall. 'On the stairway I saw someone getting butt-swiped, hit with the butt of the gun instead of being shot . . . But as he came clear at the bottom of the stairs a voice shouted, "He's got a grenade." Myself and two colleagues opened fire as soon as he came into a free-fire zone. Bang. He crumpled to the floor, he was dead. The hostages carried on through and the grenade rolled out of his hand. The pin was still in it. We continued to empty the building.'

'Prince's Gate was a turning point. It demonstrated what the regiment could do and what an asset the country had.'

Soldier J, SAS unit member

The whole siege had been broadcast live on TV to a Bank Holiday weekend audience who would normally be tuned to the final of the World Snooker Championship. The immediacy and impact of the action was gripping and the consequent interest in all aspects of the SAS was significant. Prime Minister Margaret Thatcher's analysis was succinct. 'Courage and confidence. A brilliant operation.'

The SAS insignia immediately became a sought-after badge of honour. In the weeks immediately following the Iranian embassy operation the SAS received 2,000 fresh applications from regular soldiers.

Of those 2,000, only five men subsequently passed the selection procedure.

| TEAM TALK | Pursuing a quest for the best

Individuals are the fundamental raw materials of teams and great teams are built on combinations of great individual talent. Composition – who is on the team – is the most critical determining factor of team effectiveness. You cannot win without the right individuals, but you can still lose with them. Consequently attracting, selecting and training the right talent is central to developing a top team.

Defining 'great'

Success in getting the right talent for the team starts with the absolute clarity of the team's performance challenge and common purpose. Different tasks require different types of teams and team members. Each team needs to identify what 'great' talent looks like for their specific purpose. Former world champion sumo wrestler Takanohana Kōji can be defined as great: he reached sumo's highest rank of Yokozuna and won twenty-two tournament championships between 1992 and 2001. But he is clearly less great in the context of driving a Formula 1 single-seat racing car. The right talent needs to be a good fit with a team's purpose.

In defining the calibre of talent needed to deliver superior results, high-performing teams consider the trinity of know-ledge, skills and attitudes required in the context of their spe-cific performance challenge.

Success for the SAS came from a determination of what was truly unique and distinctive, what the essence of 'great' means for an SAS trooper, given the regiment's unortho-dox doctrine of warfighting. Churchill and the SAS leaders Stirling, Mayne and Lewis painted a rich portrait of the type of soldier that they sought, demanding a distinctive defin-ition of great: individualists with the mental discipline to learn and apply the skills of teamwork and with the fortitude to balance unwavering focus on the mission objectives with the flexibility to improvise as needed.

The SAS focus on the individual and the team is fascin-ating. Many proponents of teamwork emphasize the team over the individual, slavishly repeating the office poster that 'there is no I in teamwork'. Yet the lesson from superteams is different.

Teams like the SAS focus on individual talent which has what it takes to be a champion – the selfish drive to be the best and the obsessive commitment to continuously improve. Individuals who have enough self-confidence to rely on themselves and to be able to take feedback from others. Individuals who are secure enough in themselves to be able to ask for help and see the benefit to themselves in giving help to others. Individuals who relish accountability rather than ducking it tend also to be those who are equally prepared to hold others to the high standards they set for themselves.

An essential requirement is the selection and development of individuals who have the wisdom to understand that the most self-interested act is playing the team game. These rare individuals are the lifeblood of superteams. To subvert the poster cliché, there is indeed no I in teamwork, but there *is* an I in elite . . .

The SAS determined that the right attitude was the most important variable, that being able to maintain focus under extreme pressure is imperative for mission success. Deep knowledge of strategy and expert skills are meaningless without the right state of mind. Every SAS mission is a matter of life and death, under fire and in the national interest. The Prince's Gate siege added the pressure of live television and a window of fifteen minutes to rescue the hostages. Performance in these conditions demands talent able to 'keep your head when all about you are losing theirs'.

Physical fitness is a basic necessity for the SAS, a must have, but mental toughness is the critical advantage. SAS troopers are rarely the largest or most muscular but they are typically the most resilient and determined. Given the critical importance of the right attitude and mental toughness, SAS selection is deliberately designed to be first and foremost a mental battle, a contest few applicants can win.

This is not to say that other attributes in addition to the essence of greatness do not apply, rather that a great track record of demonstrating the desired knowledge and skills is often seen as the minimum price of entry.

Attracting and selecting great team talent

Teams become magnets for talent because of their compelling core purpose and the challenge they face. 'Who dares wins' and the reputation forged in conflict make the SAS an aspiration for many in the armed forces. In addition, the very nature of an elite or special force, to be 'the best', is appealing to those who believe they have what it takes. The fact that applications increased significantly after the Prince's Gate operation is not surprising. Talent enjoys being part of a winning team.

Of course, the teams that need the greatest injections of talent are often those that are not yet winning or that find themselves on a long losing streak. Ernest Shackleton is reputed to have placed this small ad for one of his Antarctic expeditions: 'Men wanted for hazardous journey to the South Pole. Small wages, bitter cold, long months of complete darkness, constant danger. Safe return doubtful. Honour and recognition in case of success.' The response was so overwhelming that it 'seemed as though all the men of Great Britain were determined to accompany him'.

Talent seeks out an audacious challenge. For the SAS the audacious challenge lies in passing the brutal, ruthless and uncompromising high standards of selection and then in facing the most daring missions. The reputation of the Herculean labours of selection serves a dual purpose; it ensures that the vast majority of people, including most of those who might dream of being a member, do not apply while simultaneously increasing the attractiveness of joining the team to the special kind of warrior the SAS seeks to recruit. A team's brand and reputation often polarizes; it attracts the right stuff and repels the rest.

Many organizations make the mistake of basing their selection on a random series of general interviews testing for everything but the essence of greatness. It is also rare that candidates are tested on the actual tasks they will need to perform in the job and in similar conditions. High-performing teams isolate the specific essence of talent needed for superior performance and test for it ruthlessly, under as realistic performance conditions as are possible.

Maintaining the highest standards during selection training and on an ongoing basis is essential to keeping special forces . . . special. The SAS can order the return of any trooper to his original unit at any time. Membership continuously needs to be earned.

Effective selection against high standards is a key to building the trust necessary for teamwork. Diluting the team's talent pool by relaxing the standard for entry is the fastest way of destroying that team's potential for success. Low hurdles or inconsistency in the standard of selection leads to the erosion of trust between team members. In everyday work situations, as well as for the life-and-death intensity of the SAS, the belief that your colleagues are good enough is essential to collaborating with and relying on them.

Moreover, as new members are involved in recruiting, slippages in quality have rapid downward knock-on effects.

Great teams are both prepared and have the emotional maturity to pick new team members who are more capable than themselves. Rather than seeing them as a threat to status or position, existing superteam members recognize the positive challenge of having to raise their own game and the benefits of competition in the team.

Training for team excellence

Only once potential recruits pass the uncompromising standards of Test Week does the SAS begin to focus on developing and testing for the additional knowledge and skills needed to be part of an elite forces unit. The phases beyond Test Week combine selection and training and are based on the premise that with the right attitude the necessary skills can be practised and the requisite knowledge learned.

Like all great teams the four-man SAS unit encompasses all of the functional specialist skills as well as the teamwork skills, including collaboration and decision-making techniques, that the team needs to succeed. The SAS believes that this expertise, captured in the Standard Operating Procedures that underpin their actions as a team, is a unique source of competitive advantage.

As such, rather than relying on existing teamwork skills, they focus on embedding the 'SAS way' through relentless practice until it becomes second nature. Moving together as a single cohesive unit, making decisions collectively, with equality of input regardless of rank, are not natural, instinctive capabilities. These teamworking skills need to be practised, drilled, rehearsed again and again until they become new habits, and then habits which can be executed without conscious thought, instinctively. Teamwork is a high-performance habit.

Combined with Standard Operating Procedures, refined from years of application, the SAS instructors provide instruction and clear feedback to guide effective learning. A key success criterion for deliberate practice is the level of realism and experience involved. Much development of teamwork and team-building is the equivalent of learning how to swim using PowerPoint. It is fine in theory, but real practice necessitates getting into the water.

In terms of quantity, research conducted by Anders Ericsson, Professor of Psychology at Florida State University and leading researcher on expertise, popularized by Malcolm Gladwell in his influential book *Outliers*, it was the culmination of over 10,000 hours of disciplined and purposeful practice needed to become expert at any given skill. After these 10,000 hours our reactions become instinctive, and high performance becomes a habit. The SAS understands that if its members' teamwork skills are to serve as a powerful weapon, they need to be defined, trained and reviewed so often that they become reflexive. The teamwork demonstrated by the SAS to plan and execute the hostage rescue in under fifteen minutes was not the result of raw talent with gung-ho team spirit and balls of steel.

Applied purely, this principle in creating your own superteam would mean you do not need to recruit for the teamwork skill and will, but instead should focus three solid years of ten-hour days in building them. But, of course, few teams can do that.

The reality is that most teams have neither the time nor resources to train teamwork for the months and years of selection and then continuation training that the SAS applies. In commercial environments, where time is money, recruits need to hit the ground running. As such, teamwork skill and will need to be identified as part of selection and then refined with deliberate practice along-side teammates.

The Standard Operating Procedures used by the SAS are an effective means of ensuring the team can perform from the same shared script. It gives the team a basis for acting in a co-ordinated fashion proven over years of operational experience. It does not, however, trap the teams into a rigid inflexible routine. The 'fuck factor' occurs too often. The unpredictable is to be expected. The Standard Operating Procedures provide the foundation for the ingenuity and improvisation identified in SAS selection.

The SAS provides a stark contrast with many teams that rarely identify and practise teamworking skills. Senior executive teams are often the biggest culprits: they tend to combine sporadically, even reluctantly, mostly preferring to retreat to their own individual areas of responsibility where they have greater independence and control. They muddle through the core tasks of sharing information, making decisions and taking action together. There is often little clarity as to what their common and critical team tasks are, let alone a shared set of protocols for executing them. At worst they actively fight their team role. It is no surprise that they are rarely seen as a high-performing team, and even more rarely deliver as one.

But even with the strongest and best intentions about being in a team and a positive team spirit, teamwork can be poorly executed. While few teams need to operate in such extreme conditions the principles deployed by the SAS can be applied on a wider basis. The primary lesson is that teamwork is a skill that must be practised and honed. Selecting those who have a predisposition to it will ensure the training sticks more successfully and the skills become effective much more quickly.

AGENDA Pursue a quest for the best

Individuals are the building blocks of teams. Building better teams means having a focus on selecting and developing the right calibre and the right mix of team members.

Get the right calibre. When determining the right calibre of team member, the basic requirement is to look for the ability to excel at the tasks central to the team's purpose. This is typically made up of the more tangible technical and interpersonal skills and the less obvious secret ingredient of the right attitude. The right attitude for successful team players combines the love of what they do, drive, mental toughness and openness to learning that characterize top individual performers, together with a firm commitment to the team. You are looking for individuals who recognize that the relentless pursuit of their prized personal goals and ambitions is best served by being an active member of a team. The ideal team member has 'a strong but not a big ego'. They have the confidence and resilience to flourish amongst the give and take in a team. They are prepared to push their colleagues to step up yet willing to listen to feedback on their own performance in order to improve. The best team members are masters of their own role but also inspire, challenge and cajole the best from others around them. They act as multipliers of their teammates' performance.

Aim to build a team of the 'best twelve' not the 'twelve best'. Great players are necessary for victory, but a constellation of stars will still lose against a star team. Chemistry, the right mix of talent, matters in teams. A football team composed entirely of strikers – or equally only of goalkeepers – is patently absurd. Getting the right mix of skills to fulfil the team's ambitions is the minimum. You will also need to resist the temptation to build the team in your own image and ensure you have a blend of backgrounds, perspectives and personalities. Remember that your goal is not harmony but performance. Aim for a balance between the cohesion of like-minded teammates and the creative abrasion that comes from diversity. Balance also comes from hiring for both continuity and change. Fresh blood can revitalize a team, bringing in new ideas and new energy, but teams take time to become cohesive and for members to become fluent in the team's language.

Get rid of the derailers. The worst apple in a team is not the person who has poor skills. The team members who can spoil the whole barrel are those with bad team attitudes. The most challenging are those members who combine excellent skills with a selfish or destructive approach that derails team cohesion. Putting up with these anti-team players risks contagion. Some members may mimic their bad behaviour, others will lose faith in the leader's commitment to the team approach. If you want a successful team you have to abide by Manchester United manager Alex Ferguson's admirably terse law of creating a great team: 'Get rid of the c**ts.'

Promote your purpose. Finding the right talent for your team is not a popularity contest to see who has the most friends. Selection is about laser focus to separate the talent you need from everyone else. An effective common purpose will attract the talent you want and actively repel those who don't have the right stuff.

Keep standards high. Team members' trust in each other starts with confidence in their colleagues' ability to deliver at or above the required standard. Maintaining high standards in selection ensures trust between colleagues is strengthened. Upgrading talent can set a new benchmark and raise the whole team's expectations of what is good enough. One of the most certain ways of diluting your team's performance is to let selection standards slide. Allowing weaker talent to slip through the net not only reduces your overall skill level, it also sends a strongly misleading signal about the desired and expected level of capability to the rest of the team. Over time, what can start as a trickle can end in a flood: remember, first-class people hire first-class people, but second-class people hire third-class people. As the standard of incoming talent falls, the speed at which the remaining top talent leaves accelerates.

Design selection to mirror real life. Nothing beats the real thing. If you want someone who can drive fast, put him in a car and grab your stopwatch. If you need a rhythm guitarist who can weave with the lead guitar and play off the drummer, get him to audition with the band. Creating selection tests that are as close to the challenges the team face is the surest way of separating good on paper from good in practice and great in performance.

Excellence is a habit. No one and no team becomes better without practice. Team development requires its individual members to learn and grow. Developing the ability to move as a unit, with unspoken co-ordination and seamless support for each other, takes focused deliberate practice, undertaken together. Bands rehearse, the best bands rehearse the most and together, playing the music they will perform on stage. Footballers train on the pitch together, mainly by playing football. Learning as a unit by practising as a unit, in as realistic conditions as are possible and often with expert guidance, is an acknowledged process for improvement in almost every walk of team life. The most powerful process for teams to become better is to identify the most important areas where they need to collaborate, define a shared approach to working together and then practise it over and over until it becomes second nature.

'Good enough is never going to be good enough. It sounds dramatic, but what we are doing in those early days is saving lives, and you are *never, ever* going to be good enough.'

Mike Goodhand, Head of International Logistics, British Red Cross

4

THE
RED CROSS
IN HAITI
Cause and co-ordination

4.53 p.m. local time,
Tuesday, 12 January 2010, Haiti

Registering a magnitude of 7.3 on the Richter scale, and with an epicentre only 25 kilometres west of the Haitian capital Port-au-Prince, the Haiti earthquake of 2010 leaves an immediate, devastating toll: an estimated 200,000 people dead, another 300,000 injured, a quarter of a million buildings flattened or dangerously damaged, a million and a half Haitians rendered homeless. In response to the need for humanitarian assistance, the Red Cross and Red Crescent immediately move to action, activating specialist emergency relief units from around the world and launching fund-raising efforts. At St Pierre Square in Pétionville, a small suburb east of Port-au-Prince, Haitian National Red Cross Society volunteers quickly establish a first-aid station in a garage beneath the mayor's office and start treating hundreds of survivors who are shocked and dazed, many with open head wounds or crushed and broken bones. 'It's not the best place, but people are coming and we are caring for them,' says Rita Aristide, a veteran Haitian Red Cross volunteer.

At 7.30 the following morning, when Lauren Ellis, a fund-raising manager at the British Red Cross (BRC), checked her morning e-mails, she learned that the organization had already made the decision to run an appeal. By 9.00 she was in the office, orchestrating the launch of their Haiti appeal. By the end of the first day, her boss Mark Astarita had released £200,000 from the BRC's emergency funds so that immediate relief work could begin and initial pledges from corporate partners had already been secured. The Haiti appeal went on to raise £17.5 million.

The BRC's response was steered by a core team at their London headquarters, their Society Action Team, or SAT – a team of representatives from the key departments including disaster response, logistics, media and web communications and fund-raising which is run by the Head of Disaster Management. The first meeting of the SAT team for the Haiti disaster was at 10.15 a.m. that same day.

The team assessed the flow of information coming into the office, set up key decision-making teams to analyse the data and the situation, and made informed decisions under time pressure about deploying the resources available as efficiently as possible to save the maximum number of lives. Put simply, their role was disaster management, bringing organization to chaos.

The British team also had to operate within a wider web of teams. The BRC is part of, and must co-ordinate with, the International Red Cross and Red Crescent organizations. It had to balance the demands of teams on the front line and the local Haitian Red Cross with those of, amongst others, its own UK volunteer base, the interests of major fund-raisers and the demands of the media.

Immediately after the news from Haiti broke, the International Federation of the Red Cross (IFRC) had also begun mobilizing its Field Assessment and Co-ordination Team to determine the most pressing needs. Specialist emergency response teams and equipment – kept in a permanent state of readiness for just this kind of crisis – were on the ground in Haiti by the following day.

The clarity of the objective

Analysing the information contained in e-mails from the US Geological Society and breaking stories from the twenty-four-hour news channels, the leaders of the BRC recognized that, given the combination of magnitude, shallow depth and the urban location, the Haitian earthquake was going to be a major humanitarian disaster. Added to the devastating impact of the earthquake was the fact that Haiti was already one of the world's poorest countries.

From experience they knew that Haiti would have neither the infrastructure nor the economy to survive the disaster. Accelerating the more formal meeting procedures, the International Director and the Head of Fund-raising agreed, in a swift exchange of e-mails immediately after hearing the news, that the BRC had to launch their response and a fund-raising appeal. This was precisely why the Red Cross existed.

'That was the decision,' says Mike Goodhand, currently Head of International Logistics, at the time the acting Head of Disaster Management. 'It was so big and it impacted a country that was so poor, that you just knew it was going to have a huge response associated with it. To my mind it was probably the fastest launch we have ever done. It was also the clearest set of circumstances since the Indian Ocean tsunami in 2004. It was a no-brainer, if you like.'

The individuals who work and volunteer for the Red Cross and Red Crescent are governed by a shared purpose to provide help. The fundamental principles of the movement serve as a clear compass for the organization and all the people who work with it. The movement harnesses individual motivation to help and provides the most effective way for team members to do fulfilling work. Haiti sharpened the focus and motivation even further. Media and PR officer Mark South puts it like this: 'When the reason for you doing the job is on the TV twenty-four hours a day, there is no greater motivation.'

Amidst the rubble and the grieving for their own losses, the Red Cross work gave many Haitian volunteers, like Marie-Claude César Fauster, the head nurse at the Red Cross field hospital, a clear sense of purpose. 'Working in the hospital helped me to feel better. On the television we saw only dead bodies, but here I was seeing survivors and I was helping people to live. I never imagined that I would be doing something this important.'

> 'Haiti today faces a disaster of
> unprecedented proportion. We spent
> the day picking up dead bodies.'
> Wyclef Jean

In the white tented Red Cross base camp near Port-au-Prince, the sense of community was palpable. Three hundred delegates from thirty-two countries were living side by side, Iranians mingling with their Israeli fellow volunteers. People of all nationalities tried to squeeze on to the Danish table, where dinner was rumoured to be the best and a welcome relief from the diet of chocolate and rehydrated noodles.

Preparation and procedure

The situation on the ground in Haiti was – as it frequently is in the aftermath of catastrophic natural disasters – confused, chaotic and complex. So close to Haiti's capital city, the earthquake had wiped out not only basic, vital infrastructure and communication systems but also key governmental, municipal, medical and administrative buildings. The UN Stabilization Mission in Haiti suffered the largest single loss of life in any UN mission, and lost both its HQ and its mission head Hédi Annabi.

Morgues were rapidly swamped with bodies waiting for burial: Mati Goldstein, the leader of Israel's ZAKA international rescue team, painted an apocalyptic image of the scene: 'Shabbat from hell. Everywhere, the acrid smell of bodies hangs in the air. The situation is true madness, and the more time passes, there are more and more bodies, in numbers that cannot be grasped. It is beyond comprehension.'

Disasters often overload a country's existing systems. In Haiti, where the infrastructure was already weak, the earthquake destroyed all the basic services. To fill the gap and provide immediate response to the most severe and common needs on the ground, the Red Cross has developed several types of specialist emergency relief unit, or ERU. (Relief work is a sector dominated by acronyms: one textbook on the subject contains a five-page appendix of them.)

The ERUs were developed as a standardized response to the overwhelming demands of increasingly complex disasters such as the Armenian earthquake of 1988 and the massive Kurdish displacement during the first Gulf War. Initially conceived as a means of quickly delivering emergency blankets, the idea developed to create pre-trained teams of specialist volunteers and pre-packed sets of standardized equipment ready for immediate use in emergencies.

'The tsunami changed things for all
of us. It taught us how important it
is to be prepared for something on
this scale, and to know what you are
going to do when it happens.'

Sir Nicholas Young, CEO of the British Red Cross

For the Haiti disaster the Red Cross deployed ERUs to provide immediate medical treatment and preventative health
care. To cover the crucial first ten days following a disaster
the Red Cross can set up a Rapid Deployment Hospital, two
4x4 Land Cruisers and trailers containing all the necessary
medical and logistics supplies. In Port-au-Prince, four Basic
Health Care ERUs were quickly established and surgeons at
the seventy-bed field hospital ERU began operating less than
a week after the earthquake struck.

A large number of the injured required amputations
because their wounds were so badly infected. Red Cross surgeon Brynjulf Ystgaard reflected on how taking those tough
decisions was so much harder knowing the challenges survivors would face in a poor country like Haiti. The medical
ERUs were also the scenes of moments of hope: on 20 January,
following a magnitude 6 aftershock, the Red Cross field hospital helped two women give birth to healthy babies.

The Red Cross had previously positioned relief supplies
in both Haiti and nearby Panama to be available for immediate distribution in the event of a disaster. The sheer scale of

the earthquake, however, meant that supplies were hard to reach, hard to distribute and insufficient to meet the desperate needs of the survivors. The airport was severely overloaded, roads and ports compromised by the devastation. The BRC's four-person Logistics ERU team, led by Peter Pearce, focused on managing the humanitarian supply chain to ensure that incoming relief goods – of shelter, medicine, food and water, as well as other ERUs – could clear customs and then be warehoused, tracked and transported as efficiently and effectively as possible.

The La Piste camp, previously a green space in the centre of Port-au-Prince, had become a makeshift home for 10,000 people. The city's golf course had 45,000 living on it. Overall there were more than 500 such temporary camps, the inhabitants packed together with minimal shelter and little in the way of sanitation. The threat of disease in such unhygienic conditions quickly became one of the most critical risks. The BRC's expertise in this area led to the deployment of Mass Sanitation Module ERUs. Rolling out rapid latrines, flat-packed grey plastic toilets, was made more challenging by the lack of space. The latrines require deep trenches for the waste, typically dug by JCB excavators, but in Haiti there was no space for such large equipment: in many cases there was no option but to dig out the trenches by hand.

In such circumstances, clean water is essential, and the Water ERUs worked quickly to establish an alternative water treatment and distribution infrastructure. After the first three weeks over 2.5 million litres of water had been distributed – water that was cleaner than that which had been available before the earthquake.

The BRC funds their Mass Sanitation ERU and a Logistics ERU. It is also responsible for training the specialist personnel, equipping the ERUs and maintaining readiness to start deployment within six hours and be fully deployed within twenty-four. Once the units hit the ground they are designed to be self-sufficient for one month, ensuring that their focus is entirely on providing the support to the affected people.

The ERUs form a ready response, what Mike Goodhand calls a 'fixed menu', for the Red Cross to select from, based on the immediate needs on the ground. They operate in similar fashion to other elite emergency response services, with well-trained specialist personnel and standardized equipment as well as clear protocols for action, developed from real experience at the heart of previous humanitarian disasters.

Most ERU teams will not have worked together in a crisis before. There is some familiarity since many of the individuals will have come across each other in the Red Cross offices around the UK or on training programmes. It is, however, rare that they will have been deployed previously as a team.

Training for the ERUs is standard across all the Red Cross and Red Crescent national societies. It ensures that teams from the different national societies share a common understanding of what to expect and prepares members for the challenges that await them in the midst of the chaos on the ground. Mixing up the composition of the teams on each day of training allows the members to practise forming the cohesive bonds necessary for effective teamwork. Once the roster for each month is published, the team leader makes contact with each of the ERU team who are on standby. In preparation for deployment, the team will be brought together for briefing, and so that the team starts to gel.

A recently formed team in a new and distinctly challenging environment relies heavily on standard operating protocols and guidelines. Preset guidelines agreed between the national Red Cross societies and the IFRC ensure that the ERU members have a common understanding of what to do and how to do it, a critical component of teamwork. These guidelines are developed from practice in the field and synthesized by the IFRC into common approaches shared by all national societies. 'Even if we have not seen each other in six months or two years, we will fast become a great performing team,' says Mike Goodhand. 'Our ways of working are clear. You can hear it, feel it, smell it.'

The common link within a relief team is good intentions. The desire to help those who are suffering is a powerful impetus. Following Live Aid and other initiatives of the 1980s, one poll in France revealed that the ideal job of 32 per cent of the adult population was to work for Médecins Sans Frontières, whose charismatic image was described as 'swashbucklers with technical expertise'.

A robustly alternative view is given by Michael Maren, author of *The Road To Hell*, a no-punches-pulled look at humanitarian aid organizations. 'There are some really good people out there doing aid work, but I have to say that without a doubt some of the most sanctimonious assholes I have ever met . . . work for charities and aid organizations on the ground.'

Experience and competence

> 'Amidst the chaos there is in fact a
> systematic approach to provide the
> most effective and timely help possible.'
>
> Sarah Oughton, British Red Cross

In addition to the pre-packaged response, the speed and effectiveness of the BRC relief operations is driven by the experience and competence of the talent in the team.

In parallel with the first assessment team on the ground, which can take twenty-four to forty-eight hours to report back, seasoned experts within the Red Cross make their own judgements based on the pattern recognition that comes over time and with operational experience. Mike Goodhand, as acting Head of Disaster Management, instinctively realized that the densely populated and impoverished epicentre of the disaster would need medical services and safe water. After twenty years' experience of providing humanitarian relief, he intuitively understood the needs in Haiti and matched them to the tools the Red Cross had at its disposal. Immediately he began to prepare the logistics needed to get the right relief in and up and running, and the equipment and IT kit required to establish communications. His experience saved precious time in responding to the disaster.

The BRC logistics team had, between them, experience of the Bam earthquake in Iran in 2003, the Boxing Day tsunami of 2004, and the Indonesian earthquake of 2009. David Stevens brought his expertise from twenty-three years with the Royal Air Force and sixteen years with British Aerospace to ensure that much needed aid, the supplies people required to survive, could get through. For the logistics team, managing the distress of working in a disaster zone had become a way of life.

The organization has also learned that the specialist expertise of the emergency response units works best in partnership with the local Red Cross teams. The local teams in Haiti not only had more knowledge and experience of operating in their own country, they had also been responding to the emergency from the seconds after the tremors subsided.

In 2007 and 2008 Haiti was buffeted by no fewer than five hurricanes. The 2,500 Red Cross volunteers in Port-au-Prince and the other 7,500 across Haiti had been steeled by these experiences. Having learned the hard way, they were prepared to save lives in the most difficult environment. Like their countrymen, the Haitian Red Cross suffered terrible losses, but it was their experience that helped them come through. 'At first, I just couldn't accept what had happened,' says Cariolain, a thirty-one-year-old volunteer. 'It was thanks to my work as a volunteer that I was able to keep going.'

The team at the BRC also has ongoing day-to-day objectives and commitments beyond constant training. National response to emergencies, health and social care, local fund-raising events and running retail shops on the UK's high streets keep the staff and volunteers at the Red Cross fully engaged. The design of the daily activity is in many ways operational training for the exceptional major events that occur inevitably unpredictably. The ability to launch an appeal, to raise funds and manage the demands from the media is honed through practice. With six or seven appeals a year, these activities can become second nature, and business as usual is preparation for the extreme challenges of a major disaster.

Experience also ensures the team can build upon past successes and issues. The BRC had faced disasters which occurred on successive Boxing Days in 2003 and 2004 (the Bam earthquake and the Indian Ocean tsunami, respectively). So before leaving for the festive holidays in 2009, the fund-raising team members made all the necessary preparations to launch an appeal should everyone be out of the office. When the Haiti earthquake happened in early January the team were prepared and were able to move quickly.

'We are practising these skills every day for when the big one comes along. It is still a shock but we do have these automatic responses.'

Mark South, Head of Media Relations, British Red Cross

Organizing chaos: the structure
of disaster management

The Red Cross emergency relief teams on the ground faced enormous operational challenges. Chaos was the dominant leitmotif of the Haiti disaster. Damage to the control tower at Toussaint Louverture Airport hampered incoming flights. Port-au-Prince's main seaport was unusable. The public phone system was out of action, and mobile phone services disrupted. Wider elements of chaos were caused when the Prison Civile, the maximum security prison in Port-au-Prince, was destroyed and several thousand prisoners who survived the destruction escaped. Many convicts formed gangs preying on the already vulnerable and homeless people. Médecins Sans Frontières reported on 19 January that Haiti was 'like working in a war situation'.

Distributing the much needed food and supplies was a typically complex task full of unforeseen challenges. The Red Cross team dispatched to the Camp Rue du Muguet, where more than a thousand families were located, had to overcome debris scattered across the narrow steep roads leading up to the camp, compounded by mechanical problems in their vehicles.

In these difficult and dynamic situations, where delays could be fatal, the relief team's effort on the ground needed to be focused entirely on saving lives and executing the emergency response. No time could be wasted in dealing with duplication of effort or being distracted by trying to make strategic decisions. Under those conditions the operational team needed the freedom and focus to act to save lives and relieve the suffering of those impacted by the disaster.

At the Red Cross base camp, at the half-built Hilton Hotel in Port-au-Prince, the ERU team leaders' meeting was chaired by Nelson Castaño, the head of the IFRC relief operation. Each of the twenty-two ERU team heads brought clear and fast status updates. Co-ordinating the response is critical to ensure effective allocation of resources.

In London, it is the job of two key BRC teams to enable the relief effort and to support the teams in the field. They are the Society Action Team (the SAT) and the Emergency Task Force (ETF).

The SAT has a clear purpose, a fixed set of standing agenda items, and a defined attendee list including the key leaders from Communications, Fund-raising, Disaster Management and the International division. The SAT is the strategic co-ordination and decision-making body, and will meet twice a day during the intensive first week following a disaster, then daily, before the frequency of its meetings tapers off as the situation stabilizes. Away from the hectic action in a disaster zone like Haiti and the bustle of the office in the full swing of an appeal, the SAT is where the BRC leadership team shares information and makes critical strategic decisions.

The Emergency Task Force acts as the bridge between the relief teams in the field and the headquarters in London. It has a clear operational agenda to determine tactics for the BRC's response to any crisis; how to allocate funding, which teams should be mobilized, who should be put on standby and which equipment and supplies should be released. These decisions are informed by continuous updates from the teams on the ground. Decisions and operational updates are then fed upwards into the SAT meeting.

In addition to status updates from the ETF, during a disaster new data pours in from the IFRC headquarters in Geneva as well as from partners and specialist media sources such as Reuters. One member of the Disaster Management team is dedicated to managing the enormous flow of information, summarizing operational updates and stories, picking out the most critical elements and feeding them into the SAT in end-of-day bulletins. The task is essential, to spot the critical information and give the team the updates they need in the right format, 'to buffer us from the twenty-seven-page updates no one would have time to read'.

> 'In situations like this, it's always difficult to get correct information. Things change very quickly.'
>
> Emily Knox, Red Cross ERU logistics team member

The SAT meeting brings the team up to the same level of understanding of what's going on, what has been done so far and what is being planned for the future. Importantly the SAT is biased towards action, to taking decisions and breaking down tasks for the teams and volunteers to execute as soon as the meeting is finished. The SATs are purposefully calm, designed to assess progress and determine how the team can co-ordinate to achieve the objective.

Similar to standard protocols in the ERUs, the meeting's standing agenda enables the team to operate without panic, a deliberate design to go slower in order to deliver more effective decision-making, and ultimately faster action. 'The office can be going crazy on all floors, but once we go into the SAT, it is a chance to take a deep breath and look at what we are working on,' says Mark South, the Media and PR officer.

From the SAT each of the team members cascades the most relevant information through to their own teams. Lauren Ellis extracts the data most relevant to her 160 fund-raisers: information on the situation, key communication materials available for use, Q&As, how much has already been raised. For the comms teams the rule of thumb is to share as much information as possible, particularly about what has happened and what the BRC is doing about it. This information is distributed throughout the organization. For volunteers in Red Cross shops from Dumfries to Dolgellau to Dorking, the information flow means they can see the importance and need for their effort and the positive impact their work is having.

Innovation and improvisation

As much as the BRC uses preparation, protocol and process to achieve great teamwork, the very nature of disaster means that flexibility and creativity are absolutely necessary.

In responding to the Haiti disaster resources were shifted to where they were most needed with little regard for job descriptions or pecking order. Within the first three months half of the whole UK-based International division had been sent to Haiti. They included not only people who had signed up and were on the roster, but also those who were involved in long-term planning and members of the Finance department. There were no 'it's not in my job description' complaints or parochial defensiveness.

Standing in a temporary camp that was covered in human excrement, Peter Pearce and David Peppiatt, Director of the International division, were presented with visceral evidence of the need to revise the BRC's strategy, with a full focus on mass sanitation taking priority over providing shelter programmes and work to kick-start the economy.

Haiti also saw the BRC innovate in the communications arena. As Charles Williams, the editorial manager, explained, it was the first 'social media' disaster, with Twitter and Facebook providing supporters and members with a direct connection: 'It created a huge opportunity to serve an enormous audience with very frequent updates.'

In Haiti the Red Cross used SMS texts to reach people with practical, simple messages focused on health and weather, such as how to prepare your shelter when a hurricane is coming. In partnership with Trilogy International Partners, who owned the Voilà network in Haiti, 50 million SMS messages were sent in the year after the disaster, helping Haitians with practical life-saving advice such as understanding how to prevent cholera through simple hygiene routines. The Red Cross also focused on restoring families separated by the disaster, with over 25,000 people registering through its website.

Technology was also used by the BRC's fund-raising team, who launched the 'text to give' initiative. In America this campaign raised over $1 million in three weeks. Traditionally, fund-raising generates 50 per cent of donations within the first two weeks of a disaster. The scale of Haiti and the media attention saw donations continuing to increase after four weeks.

Cultural values and principles

Team meetings at the BRC can get heated – not surprisingly, given the high stakes involved in humanitarian crises and the fact that team members are fiercely passionate about what they do. 'What you have is a bunch of people who are technically extraordinarily competent in their field of emergency response, recovery and risk reduction and, yes, they bat their side, and they bat it with a lot of knowledge and passion,' observes Mark Goodhand.

Yet the debate never descends into vindictive or personal attacks. No one can recall voices being raised. The Red Cross has respect for human dignity as a core value, which applies to the members of the leadership team in London as much as it does to those who need emergency relief. The discussions are difficult to resolve because there is so much respect for different viewpoints.

The acid test of values is that teams remain true to them even when the cost of holding to such beliefs is high. The Haitian Red Cross was devastated by the earthquake, every single member affected, losing relatives and close friends, some losing their own lives. Like their country, the Haitian society did not have the strongest capacity before the disaster, but the BRC would never ask the locals to step aside even when it was clear the BRC had greater capacity, training and resources. Instead, a key aspect of the BRC work was to support and strengthen the role of the national society and the involvement of Haitians in rebuilding their own country.

The Haitian Red Cross and their international ERU colleagues are capable of delivering more as a team than either could alone. The combination of local knowledge and specialist skills allowed the Red Cross to deliver life-saving aid without having to rely on armed guards even in the most violent and destitute areas. 'We don't use barbed wire or armed security,' says one IFRC team leader. 'We rely on our emblem and the goodwill people have for the Haitian Red Cross.'

When doing good is not necessarily good *enough*

In the Red Cross movement, especially in its response to the disaster in Haiti, cause and motivation were never in question. Everyone wanted to do the right thing.

Team members simply want to be the best at what they do. Like many professionals, they value the opinion of their colleagues most of all and peer respect is an important foundation for both pride and a genuine sense of mutual accountability. Nobody wants to be the one who drags the team down. When things go wrong, the team is prepared to ask difficult questions of itself. A team discussion regarding the reason behind a lack of success in raising funds for humanitarian relief during the Pakistan conflict in 2009 was characteristically uncomfortable.

Like other high-performing organizations, the BRC is target-driven. The ERUs have time targets for deployment, as do fund-raising launches; the return on investment from marketing activity is measured, as are the advertising value equivalents of media coverage and the number of social media 'friends'.

The BRC also benchmarks itself continuously against respected competition. When Oxfam or Save the Children does something innovative, the first question asked by the BRC is 'Why didn't *we* do that?' As with champion sportsmen and women, the desire to improve continuously is also a feature of those who work for the BRC. They constantly question how they could have reacted better or faster, how they could have been more prepared, predicted smarter. The BRC's combination of professional pride and core purpose delivers a real performance edge.

Leadership

The BRC team demonstrates real versatility in leadership style. During the quieter periods between disasters, leadership is conducted democratically, with much focus on helping the next generation of leaders to rise through the ranks.

However, as a disaster unfolds, the leaders adopt a more autocratic style, a style which their teams both appreciate and demand from them. In the face of the time pressure there is simply not enough time for consensus. People want clarity about what they need to do, a series of straightforward and simple tasks. Collectively the team combines to deliver what staff members call an 'unfaltering belief in what the Red Cross is doing'.

Interacting with volunteers and supporters requires yet another form of leadership, one based on inspiring in people a desire to help and then enabling them to do so. In Haiti, the leaders had to adjust their leadership style when interacting with the other aid agencies. Goodwill and positive influence were needed to co-ordinate the multiple organizations. Command and control was not an option.

Disaster management has several distinct phases: relief, recovery, and risk reduction. The BRC efforts in supporting

Haiti in the emergency relief phase demonstrated superteam performance. Disaster response is a sprint but disaster recovery is a marathon. After the immediate emergency work, the BRC began the long road to recovery. They are still there today. Some of the work they are doing, like building sewage systems, will be far better and more resilient than the original infrastructure.

Pierre Marie Gérard, a Haitian Red Cross volunteer helping build hurricane-resistant housing, represents the optimistic forward-looking attitude: 'Despite the awfulness of the quake, I feel excited about the possibility of building a new Haiti. My dream is a new Haiti.'

In the first year after the earthquake, the Red Cross movement delivered over a million relief items including blankets, tarpaulins and mosquito nets, reached over 288,000 people with health services and was producing and distributing close to 2 million litres of clean water a day. With twenty-one Emergency Response Units (ERUs) deployed, thirty-three national societies mobilized and around six hundred volunteers and delegates from around the world, in addition to the local volunteers, the Haiti earthquake response was the largest single-country mobilization in the history of the International Red Cross and Red Crescent movement.

Yet the reality is that, even two years on from the disaster, many Haitians are still living in tents. The dream of a new Haiti remains at many levels unfulfilled: a stark reminder that while disaster response can be extremely effective, disaster recovery is an even more complex business.

TEAM TALK Shaping the environment for success

The Red Cross deals in disasters. The most powerful reflection from the Red Cross emergency operation in Haiti is that great teamwork can save lives. The work of the BRC team, their Haitian colleagues and their colleagues from across the movement is often the difference between life and death, hope and suffering. The Red Cross clearly demonstrates the idea that just doing good is not good enough. The team has a strong conviction that they offer the most effective response to humanitarian disasters, a professional pride rooted in the drive to achieve. The goal of the Red Cross is an effective combination of doing the right thing and doing it right.

The speed and depth of the Red Cross's response was based on the team's ability to balance almost paradoxical elements. Preparation and procedure based on significant learning from experience was combined with improvisation and innovation. Steady and deliberate decision-making was married to intense, immediate operational execution. Strong values and fundamental principles were mixed with a competitive drive to deliver more, faster and better. The leadership style flexed between being autocratic, collaborative and acquiescent, to fit the situation and the team's needs.

Providing effective emergency relief in the face of devastation, chaos and complexity, the BRC team highlights the importance of 'controlling the controllables'. They made a concerted effort to shape those elements of their operating environment that they could affect. In particular they focused on defining the right structure, resources and relationships to ensure the team had the best chances of success.

Situations of high pressure and complexity requiring urgent decision-making and rapid action create tough conditions for individuals to perform in. The need to operate collectively in such circumstances is even more challenging. The choreography needed for a team to launch a fund-raising appeal, to work with the media to get the message out, to deploy specialist emergency relief units and to partner with local volunteers and a disaster zone several thousand miles away would be challenging in a 'normal' environment. To do so when every second counts and lives are at stake requires a clear, shared approach, an approach based on proven, practical experience, and understood and practised by the whole team until it becomes second nature.

Team structure: clarifying team roles

The BRC has evolved an approach to team structure to deal with disasters. It has defined the everyday tasks that form business as usual, as well as the essential tasks that need to be executed in responding to an emergency like the Haiti earthquake. Individual roles within the team are tightly defined and clarified, leaving no confusion as to who is accountable for what, whether media relations, fund-raising efforts or logistics. Clarity of individual roles and responsibilities is the basis for ensuring everything that needs to get done actually gets done by the most qualified and often specialist resource.

A lack of clarity or ill-defined roles and responsibilities is a common failing amongst teams. For individuals, role ambiguity tends to increase stress and job dissatisfaction. When individuals are unclear about what their role entails and what is expected of them in a team environment they can waste precious time and energy fighting to defend their own turf or trying to untangle who does what. Poorly defined roles and responsibilities in a team can mean uneven balances in workload. Critical tasks are missed and others are duplicated. Lack of clarity regarding team roles is a principal source of friction and conflict in teams and can result in the whole becoming *less* than the sum of the parts.

Effective role clarity specifies who is responsible for what and, importantly, how the individual roles fit together as part of the whole.

In meeting the overwhelming challenges of Haiti the BRC team combined clarity of individual roles with an understanding of what others in the team contributed. That overview of the whole team helped team members understand how they fitted in and the importance of their contribution. It also enabled team members to provide backup beyond their core role when the task demanded it. Given the scale of the Haiti disaster, it was all hands on deck.

The structure used by the Red Cross provided a solid foundation that allowed for improvisation. Disaster situations are so fluid that improvisation is always required. Unlike bureaucracies, where roles become ossified and mindsets fixed, the BRC uses clear role structure as the starting point for teamwork. As with the SAS's four-man unit, team members have their own responsibilities, but are also prepared to go beyond their own role boundaries in support of each other and the team objectives.

In addition to role clarity within the team, the BRC also clearly defined the roles of the different teams in responding to the crisis. The Society Action Team meeting and the Emergency Task Force meeting each had its own distinct mandate, responsibilities and clear standing agenda. This definition ensured that the meetings were focused on the task at hand and that no time or effort was wasted in redesigning the wheel or in duplicating discussions.

The BRC also structured the team to make considered decisions while maintaining momentum. The SAT meetings delivered the calm reflective environment necessary to consider and determine the best strategy. The Red Cross used the SAT to define not just direction but as a mechanism to plan communication and execution, in a way that accelerated implementation outside the meeting room.

Having the right people around the table ensured the team

had access to all the expertise needed to share information and make decisions. Importantly, involving the team members who are responsible for execution in the decision-making process increases their commitment to deliver.

Team structure, team size

A key aspect of team structure is the size of the team. The BRC endeavours to limit team membership to those necessary to fulfil the objectives of the meeting. As Pixar did, it seeks to gather information and input from many but keeps its decision-making team small. In Haiti, the Emergency Relief Units were as small as their mission objectives allowed. The logistics team had four members, the same number as the basic SAS unit, the smallest number possible to include all the requisite skills needed to operate in a difficult environment.

Larger groups are used for information-sharing and co-ordination, such as the update meetings in the base camp near Port-au-Prince, but for decision-making and operational action, team size is kept deliberately small.

Teams need to guard against a natural tendency to grow beyond the most effective size. It is seductive to believe that adding more resources to the team will make it easier to meet a challenge. In situations where there are multiple stakeholders, it is tempting to think that every interest group must be represented on the team. Equally, especially in leadership teams, seniority is considered to confer automatic inclusion. Membership may even be granted as a reward, with no thought to suitability, since successful teams are often clubs people want to belong to.

However, there is considerable research demonstrating that while productivity initially increases as individuals join the team, beyond a certain size productivity begins to deteriorate. Team effectiveness, especially in decision-making teams, tends to deteriorate above a dozen members, although the tipping point might be as low as nine. As the number of team voices increases, focus is harder to maintain. Diversity of opinion is useful in smaller groups, but in larger groups it can make agreement impossible. Co-ordinating a large team can become a time-intensive process in itself, detracting from the team's core mission.

Prioritizing resources

Two centuries ago Dominique Jean Larrey, a surgeon in Napoleon's army, came up with the battlefield idea of triage, a system of prioritizing casualties in which the order of events is: get in, stabilize the wounded, decide which is the most life-threatening condition and deal with that first. Everything else waits until later on, but that everything else can't be forgotten; it still needs to happen. Modern-day disaster response teams operate along much the same lines. Few teams, and especially those reliant on volunteers and donations, have all the resources they would like, and as such the skill comes from doing more with less. Crisis quickly clarifies the 'need to have' and the 'nice to have'. Like triage on the battlefield, it forces the prioritization of scarce resources.

In determining how to be effective with limited resources the BRC made the most of one of the most important assets for all teams: information. As soon as the information regarding the earthquake was received the team had the experience to translate news into action. They knew it would be necessary to launch an appeal and a rescue effort immediately. Having the right information to appreciate what was happening in Haiti, in Geneva and in the fund-raising efforts across Britain was critical in shaping the team's actions.

Information is vital, and communicating it is essential, but it must also be communicated in a useful manner. Too much information can be as difficult to manage as too little, and it takes considerable skill to balance quality and quantity. The Red Cross sets out to refine the information into data-driven insights that are both meaningful and actionable – meaningful in the sense of materially important to the mission, actionable in the sense that the team can do something practical about them.

High-level strategic decision-making in the SAT meeting worked best when combined with direct input and insight from the front line. David Peppiatt had to stand in a field of excrement to fully appreciate where the BRC's scarce resources would have the biggest impact. As the US Marines' doctrine of warfighting says, operational decisions 'should be taken as close as possible to the enemy'.

A further source of insight came from past performance. Over the years, the Red Cross has been able to identify patterns of action that have worked well, mistakes commonly made and issues that need to be resolved perennially. Experience is an effective teacher.

Its worldwide network enables the Red Cross to channel and spread experience and ideas rapidly and effectively across the globe. The ERUs are a good example of such an approach, codified from the challenging experiences of emergency relief in Pakistan, Kenya and Thailand. By pre-packaging the supplies, equipment and personnel they knew would be needed in a ready-to-mobilize form, the Red Cross improved both the speed and the quality of its response – effectively doing more with less.

The individuals in the ERUs are prepared and trained to work together as a team, guided by approaches refined from the deep reservoirs of the movement's experience and expertise in relief work. Like the approaches, the equipment is standardized, ensuring the kit could be used by any of the different ERU teams.

Time is a further important resource that teams need to manage effectively. The decision to launch immediately and the readiness of the ERUs allowed the BRC to move quickly. The notion of 'going slow to go fast' can also be seen in the level of preparation the SAS committed to the Iranian embassy siege, so that their rescue could be decisive in less than twenty minutes. Superteams follow the maxim of investing the time upfront in preparation, with the return on that investment coming from speed and effectiveness in execution. As with the old maxim, time spent sharpening the axe pays off in cutting down the trees.

Team relationships

The Red Cross movement also defined a clear structure to enable the co-ordination of the different teams from the multiple national societies, including the Haitian Red Cross, into a community of purpose. All other teams work in partnership with and at the invitation of the local society, in this instance the Haitian Red Cross.

Here the design of the organization also reflects the wider common purpose. The relief is not given *to* the affected population but carried out *with* them. The Red Cross approach is fundamentally enabling; to help those affected by disaster to help themselves.

The way that the Red Cross emergency relief is executed has a critical impact on the recovery process and also in ensuring greater resilience against future disasters. The local volunteers working alongside their international colleagues in the ERU hospitals retain the skills they have learned in working with the Red Cross and are better prepared for future crises.

AGENDA Shape the environment for success

Creating the conditions for your team to deliver better results means structuring the team effectively, in terms of its size and roles, and managing the resources and relationships it needs to be successful.

Keep teams as small as the mission allows. The promise of teams lies in their ability to deploy greater numbers and a broader set of skills and represent a broader mix of perspectives. It is therefore not surprising that many teams fall into the trap of adding increasing numbers of people to the team. As teams grow, however, so does the challenge of co-ordinating them, getting agreement and building cohesion. Research suggests that if it contains fewer than four members the group may not be big enough to capture the potential benefits of teams. Above twelve members and those benefits may be outweighed by the costs of social complexity. Where team size is an option, less will deliver more. Smaller teams make it easier to forge common purpose, build bonds between members and choreograph collaboration.

Clarify roles within the team. To get the most out of your team you need to make sure that each member has three levels of clarity about team roles. (1) They need to know what is expected of them and why it matters. Such clarity goes beyond defining a role in terms of its responsibilities and the limits of its authority and decision rights; it also means connecting how each role contributes to the team's common purpose. (2) Team members need a practical understanding of the other roles and how they add value to the team. Role swapping has been demonstrated to improve results as it embeds the understanding of how the co-ordination works from the other members' perspective and increases the likelihood of empathetic responses and mutual support. (3) Team members need to know how the pieces of the puzzle fit together and appreciate their interdependence. Only with all three levels of clarity can individuals make the transition to operating as a unit.

Ensure the organization is as level as it can be. Your goal is to protect your team from unnecessary layers and make your team agile in responding to changing events. Reducing hierarchy can deliver a freer flow of information, ideas and feedback. You should not, however, discount the benefits of having a final authority. There is always a moment when a leader is needed to cut through the Gordian knots which teams can tie themselves into.

Be flexible within a framework. Team structure – the size, roles and boundaries of a team's authority – will give you the platform for your team's performance. But you should treat structure like Keith Richards' view of a song: as a coat hanger on which he can hang a different shirt every time he plays, weaving new melodies with Ronnie Wood. Structure should form the basis, not the barrier, to improvisation and teamwork.

Control the controllables. So much in a team's environment is beyond the team's control. Rather than trying to change the weather, focus your team's energy on the elements that they can affect, no matter how small. Being obsessive and detailed in preparation, improving tiny aspects here and there, has a cumulative impact that can add up to a winning edge.

Focus on resources that are fit for purpose. Time, information, the right equipment and financial capital – resources are always in short supply. As you grapple with the need to do more with less, you must ruthlessly prioritize the resources that are vital to your team's progress and shed any excess baggage. If in doubt, investing in the right people and their resourcefulness is the most effective way to secure the assets your team needs to succeed.

Build bridges beyond the team. Every team has important links with the outside world. Cohesive teams, even those with a common enemy, should not retreat to become islands. Reaching out to other individuals, groups and organizations is an important source of support and resources that your team may not possess. Identifying who to engage with and building productive relationships is a team task. Speaking with one voice, communicating a consistent unequivocal message, will enable your team to maximize its influence.

'The Rolling Stones is a vehicle that only works when we put it in motion.'

Ronnie Wood

5

THE
ROLLING STONES
Creativity and consistency

Saturday, 18 February 2006,
Rio de Janeiro, Brazil

During the Rolling Stones' Bigger Bang tour of 2005–7, for one night only, on the expanse of Rio's Copacabana beach, 1.5 million fans gather to watch the Stones perform a free concert – one of the largest gigs the world has ever seen. The stage, specially constructed and facing Sugar Loaf Mountain, is the height of a seven-storey building, with an aerial walkway giving the band direct access from their hotel just across the road. Eight additional sound towers have been constructed along the length of the beach to cope with the size of the audience. It is a show which marks one of the pinnacles of the band's lengthy career, and which sums up the extraordinary logistical and creative operation of the team around them which delivers high and above all consistent levels of performance night after night.

As the Rolling Stones and their immediate entourage crossed the high walkway linking their hotel to the stage, even these battle-hardened veterans were impressed by the size of the crowd stretching into the distance. 'The audience was a mile long,' remembers Ronnie Wood. 'It was overwhelming.' They all felt a heightened buzz that night.

On stage, Keith Richards used the same quip that he has been using for years at gigs all around the world: 'It's good to be here. It's good to be anywhere . . .' His throwaway line contains a significant truth, though. Despite the fact that Keith and his fellow Stones have put themselves through more experiences than most other human beings (novelist Carl Hiaasen, a Stones fan, once remarked, 'Holy moly. Whatever Keith has in his DNA should be distilled and made immediately available to the general public') they turn in world-class performances at each show on each leg of each world tour they undertake.

At that point the band were all aged over sixty – bar Ronnie Wood, whose sixtieth birthday would not be celebrated until the following year. Their ability to reproduce that level of consistency derives from the way they have constructed their interaction as a group of four musicians, and from the people and the apparatus – the management, touring personnel, procedures and attitude – which surrounds, supports and sustains these four men. The STP, the Stones Touring Party, as it was first dubbed on their American tour of 1972, is a team designed to deliver the artists, the Rolling Stones ('the principals'), to the stage intact, in tune and ready to rock 'n' roll.

Family – cohesion and conflict

> 'Mick is my wife, whether I like it
> or not. We can't get a divorce.'
> Keith Richards

The Rolling Stones have often been described in terms of family. Keith Richards frequently jokes that Mick Jagger is the Pop while he is the Mom. And as with any marriage of strong personalities, their union has had its moments of tension as well as of great togetherness.

Others have described the pair as siblings. They call themselves 'The Glimmer Twins' for their production credits. The relationship is that of close brothers, but ones who frequently disagree.

But it is the similarities and differences that are at the heart of their half-century of cohesiveness. When the Stones started out in 1962, what bonded them was their love of R&B. Mick and Keith had first started talking on the platform of Dartford station when Keith noticed Mick was carrying a copy of the album *The Best of Muddy Waters*. In the following days they discovered they shared a powerful passion for R&B, and during evenings at the Marquee Club and the Ealing Club they met others drawn to the same music, including Charlie Watts, Brian Jones and Ian Stewart, who, though never an official Rolling Stone (their first manager Andrew Loog Oldham didn't think he fitted the look of the band), remained part of the team as road manager and stage pianist until his death in 1985.

The shared musical heritage and passion for playing is the Stones' taproot. None of the band, it seems, ever tires of music. Certainly for Keith it consumes every aspect of his life, from morning to night. The love of rock 'n' roll has endured despite the alternative temptations and distractions of sex and drugs through the decades.

That shared musical passion persists, especially between Ronnie and Keith, comrades in guitars. Ronnie is still 'the new boy', even though he has been in the Stones three times longer than his predecessors Brian Jones and Mick Taylor combined. The two of them play off each other in ways that push and pull them both to explore new musical frontiers within the framework of music they have been playing together for years. They call this the 'ancient form of weaving'.

Everything the two guitarists do together goes into the mix: the shared history of extraordinary adventures, discussions about the music they love, snooker games backstage, the seemingly mundane routines of preparation and the simmering tensions, too. Brewing constantly over the decades, this alchemy continues to produce a freshness that keeps the Stones' concert performances relevant even after half a century.

In the early days, the band not only had their common musical bond, but had lived together – Keith, Mick, Charlie and Brian Jones shared a 'beautiful dump' in Chelsea's Edith

Grove – and had been crammed together in the back of Ian Stewart's van to traipse between gigs, squished into some old aircraft seats, with their amps and drum kit pressing up against them.

Later they would spend intense time together in the South of France recording *Exile on Main Street* when they had to leave the UK for tax reasons. Ronnie Wood identifies both the taxman and various record company execs as common enemies who also helped bind the band together, along with an Englishness (underlined when they were out of the country) and a strong sense of humour.

As important in the group's chemistry were the differences between the band members. While Mick brings drive to the band and provides an organizing force and momentum, Keith is its spirit. Mick has a clear vision and an end point in mind, whereas Keith is much looser, happy to allow ideas to marinate for years. 'I never plan anything,' Keith says. 'Mick needs to know what he's doing tomorrow. I'm just happy to wake up. Mick's Rock. I'm Roll.' These differences are, it seems, central to their creativity. They bounce off each other in ways that both recognize as a magnetic pull.

As an example of Mick's desire to control, there is a telling sequence in the Martin Scorsese documentary *Shine a Light*, recorded in 2006 at the Beacon Theatre in New York. Right up to the last moment, Mick will not tell Scorsese, this Oscar-winning, legendary director, what the set list is going to be, even though Scorsese needs to know to plan his camera angles. Even the rest of the band just have to wait.

During the 1980s, the band nearly imploded as a result of the clash between Mick's Rock and Keith's Roll. At one point there was a distinct possibility they might never play together again. Essentially, Mick felt that he as lead vocalist would be more likely to succeed as a solo artist. Keith believed in the power of the band, and that he was central to it. Factions were formed, bad blood flowed. Only on the very brink of the precipice were both of them persuaded to step back. Ronnie had not been prepared to let the band wither. His enthusiasm is an irresistible part of his character, and with the instinct of a veteran peace negotiator, he understood that putting the two back together meant getting them to talk: 'Once they get talking, they will hack it out.' By playing middleman and acting as telephone switchboard, Ronnie facilitated an end to the feud and secured the basis for the Stones meeting together as a group after a two-year hiatus.

It is not just Mick and Keith who have had their battles. Charlie tells the story of how, one night in the 1980s, he had a phone call from Mick, who'd been out drinking with Keith, effectively saying, 'Where's my drummer?' Charlie, dapper as ever, strode upstairs to Mick's hotel room and punched the lead vocalist, telling him never to call him that again. He regrets the episode now, but it points up the emotions that can be stirred up even in the most rock-solid band member.

The Rolling Stones are, despite the band's longevity, a fragile apparatus. A couple of weeks after the Copacabana show in 2006, Keith Richards famously tumbled out of a palm tree on holiday in Fiji, causing the cancellation of a number of shows on that leg of the *Bigger Bang* tour. Mick Jagger's vocal cords have become, not surprisingly, far less resilient over recent years, again leading to a higher percentage of rearranged dates during the course of tours. Without every member of the Stones in place, the show, literally, cannot go on.

Only at one point in their history was that ever any different.

When Keith Richards was sentenced for heroin possession in Canada in 1977, there was a strong possibility that, although a jail sentence was avoided by some deft footwork and a posse of expensive lawyers, he might not be able to return to North America for many years. The contract with the record company and promoters had to be adjusted to state that the 'Rolling Stones', for the purposes of fulfilling the contract, would be Mick Jagger and any other three of the band (Bill Wyman was still a member at the time). Keith Richards was devastated, but had to accept that it was his own activities that threatened to destabilize the band.

The individual band members have come to realize that it is something in the balance, the chemistry, the alchemy between them which provides the edge and the energy – and in fact that their very difference is the key factor.

Charlie Watts says of Mick and Keith, 'They are as close now as they were when they were kids, and as different in their ways as when they were nineteen. The only thing that brought us all together was the fact that we were trying to play in a band.' As Charlie also observes, the band are 75 per cent separated but 100 per cent together.

> 'We need each other and when one of us is alone, there's something missing.'
>
> Ronnie Wood

Reinventing the business of rock 'n' roll

Mick Jagger is more than the lead singer in the Rolling Stones. On stage he is a great showman, a natural entertainer able to captivate huge audiences under his spell. But Jagger also has an alert business brain, as a fifty-year veteran of the music industry, and learns from every deal, good or bad. His interest in the Stones as a commercial enterprise reflects his experience and sharp intellect. A key aspect of this insight is his understanding that the Rolling Stones have several distinct businesses within their overall portfolio. 'They all have income streams, they have different business models, they have different delegated people that look after them. And they have to interlock,' says Jagger.

Much of the Rolling Stones' business success has been based on the financial wizardry, behind the scenes, of Prince Rupert Loewenstein, described by Keith Richards as the mastermind behind their set-up. In 1968 Mick Jagger brought in the then merchant banker to review the Stones' finances as he could not understand how their success with fans was not being translated into cash in their pockets. Turning round their fortunes, literally, in the 1970s, Loewenstein established a structure around the band that maximizes profits by 'interlocking' the different aspects of their business together through four companies each focusing on a specific area of business: touring, publishing, records and image, and merchandising rights.

As well as rethinking the business end, the Rolling Stones have made a habit of reinventing the rock concert and the rock tour. In the early days, it was jumping from venue to venue, without sounds or lights or anything. But from 1969 onwards the band were travelling with their own staging, lights and sound equipment. The tours were infamous for the band's performances as much as for the never-ending high jinks and after-show parties. But until Prince Rupert took a firm grip on the touring finances, the tours were never lucrative for the band members. As Jagger pointed out, 'Obviously there was someone who made money, but it certainly wasn't the band.' Loewenstein's long relationship with the band typifies their ability to surround themselves with a team of trusted, talented, long-serving people who provide continuity even when, or especially when, the band members themselves may be somewhat disjointed. Alan Dunn, tour manager and logistics guru since 1968, says, 'Continuity is the whole success.' That wider team also amplifies the Stones' cohesion and their harmony, and helps muffle and diffuse any discord.

Things changed further with the *Steel Wheels/Urban Jungle* tour of 1989–90, when Canadian promoter Michael Cohl joined the Rolling Stones' close-knit team. For previous tours Cohl had promoted the Stones concerts in Canada, reporting to Bill Graham, the tour director hired by the Stones. The system, used by most bands, had the tour director organizing individual deals with local promoters who cut deals with venues in each city where the band would play. Typically a promoter received 10–15 per cent of ticket sales after the cost of the show, and the tour director would be responsible for collecting the tour revenue promoter by promoter.

Cohl offered something different. He proposed being a one-stop shop, offering the Rolling Stones $40 million for forty shows. He would book the entire tour, including dealing with venues directly and cutting out the local promoters. Central to the deal was introducing or amplifying other tour revenue streams to reflect the Stones' passionate and broad fan base; skyboxes with seats practically on top of the stage, bus tours, bigger TV deals, more styles and more integrated merchandising as well as corporate sponsorship. Having one point of co-ordination for the whole tour enabled the various streams to cross-pollinate and for their impact to add up to more than the sum of the individual parts.

Mick Jagger's advisers and his business savvy meant the band focused on the costs as well as the top-line opportunities for the band's touring. The bad deals and restrictive contracts of the Stones' early years were powerful teachers. Jagger's starting assumption is that few showbusiness organizations are well run, that too much money is always paid out and so the tour is over budget before it even starts. He has powerful formulas in his mind, learned over time, about how many dates the band will be into a tour before it breaks even.

Steel Wheels/Urban Jungle grossed over $260 million, a record at the time. The *Voodoo Lounge* tour of 1994–5 brought in $370 million, *Bridges to Babylon/No Security* took $390 million. *A Bigger Bang* generated $550 million, selling 4.5 million tickets (plus another million and a half audience at the free concert on Copacabana beach). The formula clearly works.

Creating space to breathe

The band retain their freshness by coming together only when the occasion demands: they want to record a new album, or they are going out on tour. When they and the core tour party meet again after two or three years away, there is genuine pleasure in getting back together. Ronnie Wood says it is 'like a war veterans' reunion'.

> 'The Stones still work. It always comes easy once you get the bunch of guys together. It's the getting the guys together that's the hard part.'
>
> Keith Richards

When the band are not touring or recording, they lead separate lives. The days of hanging out together, living in a dodgy flat, sharing a van, are long gone. As Mick says, 'When you're not on the road you can give a lot more attention to your family than someone in a nine-to-five job that stays late at the office . . . You've got maybe two months when your time is very much your own. This is a very ruthless life if you're on your own. The only thing you've got to hang on to is family.'

Each member of the Rolling Stones has pursued individual musical projects: Charlie has his jazz big band, Keith jams with the New Barbarians. At times these have been seen as distractions or threats to the band. Certainly they have the potential to add to the tension. Paradoxically, though, they have been an important aspect of cohesion, allowing the members to explore different and more personal passions without having to leave the group.

The enforced downtime between the tours has enabled the band to focus on other personal projects, including opportunities beyond music, such as Ronnie Wood's career as an artist and Mick Jagger's film production company. The gaps allow space for the sense of occasion and audience desire to build again.

Once a new tour is pencilled in Mick Jagger and Charlie Watts combine to focus on stage design and merchandising, Jagger conceiving of the Stones' concerts in similar terms to the three or four acts of a theatrical production, and drawing on his long-held fascination with the stage designs of Cecil Beaton, the architecture of Frank Lloyd Wright and Santiago Calatrava, or film-set work such as John Beard's designs for the movie *Brazil*. He is generally more concerned than the other members of the band, whom he refers to as 'the musicians', with the showmanship and the staging, the platform that releases his ability to connect with the audience.

Working regularly with Jagger and Watts has been architect and set designer Mark Fisher, who, alongside Patrick Woodroffe, the lighting designer, has collaborated with the Stones since the *Steel Wheels* tour. Initial ideas for the *Bigger Bang* tour focused on placing the band in an 'operatic' environment, evolving the design from a grand nineteenth-century opera house into the final design, which had portions of the audience on sweeping balconies at the back of the stage, either side of a giant LED video screen. Fisher describes their work as 'guerrilla architecture'. 'In a sense, it's a matter of transforming a football stadium into a temple for a night. This is an instant popular opera enacted on a huge scale.'

Given the band's status as, still, the biggest rock 'n' roll live band in the world, each new tour launch is a media event. Over the years these events have acted as tangible, physical proof and one of the few visible signs the band were still together.

As with previous tours, *A Bigger Bang* was launched in New York, where for the 1975 tour launch the band performed 'Brown Sugar' on the back of a flatbed truck driving through Manhattan, with a growing gaggle of fans stopping traffic across the city. More than thirty years later, the band launched the *Bigger Bang* tour with a live set from the balcony of the Juilliard School of Music, introducing a new song ironically entitled 'Oh No, Not You Again'.

The Stones rented out the whole of a large Toronto school for their *Bigger Bang* rehearsals. They have used Toronto as a rehearsal base for many years, so much so that Alan Dunn remembers arriving there 'and the street people knew my first name'. They created a full concert set-up, complete with dressing rooms, canteen, offices and studios as well as converting the gym into the actual rehearsal arena. Rehearsals are the opportunity for the band to re-form, to find their collective rhythm and make the transition from everyday life into the nomadic charge of the Stones on tour.

As a consequence of their long and prolific career the Stones have a large body of work; twenty-nine studio albums and ten live albums with ninety-two singles. There is so much material that even Keith and Mick, the songwriting team, often forget exactly how some of their work goes, and rely on long-time sideman, keyboardist Chuck Leavell, who is the chronicler and guardian of a comprehensive archive of all the different arrangements and set lists the Stones have used on previous tours. For the *Bigger Bang* tour they practised to perfection nearly a hundred tunes, honing their ability to play them to the very high standard the band set for themselves.

Mick takes the lead on defining the set list. Songs were chosen to reflect the different venues the Stones would play on the tour, ranging from the tour-launching club nights through to the larger arena and stadiums. Mick might want to open up the set with 'Start Me Up', because it was totally obvious; Keith would not for precisely the same reason. Once the *Bigger Bang* set list was finally agreed, the band marked it up on a large canvas on the stage and Ronnie turned it into a work of art by painting around the list, making it a central reference point during rehearsals.

The *Bigger Bang* tour started, as is the Stones' tradition, with a club performance, at the Phoenix Concert Theatre in Toronto. Mick Jagger has always maintained that a more intimate performance is the best way to kick off any tour. The pent-up energy, especially after all the tension of the build-up and the concentrated rehearsing, is unleashed into the confines of a small venue and the interaction with the audience is electric.

Early tours were rehearsed around a fixed set list with minimal changes made as the tour progressed. But for the *Forty Licks* tour of 2002–3, celebrating the band's fortieth anniversary, the Stones began to play around with the set list, changing up to four or five songs every night. *A Bigger Bang* continued to see the nightly changes in the set list, adding to the freshness of each performance. 'We want every concert to be better than the last one,' says Ronnie Wood.

By the end of the *Bigger Bang* tour, the Rolling Stones had played 2,637 songs, including 81 different numbers. 'Jumpin' Jack Flash', often the song which opened the show, had been performed the most at 133 times. By way of contrast, some songs were played only once, frequently reflecting a local flavour: Jimmy Webb's 'Wichita Lineman' and Marty Robbins' 'El Paso' were played only in those two cities, for example.

A life on the road

To spend over two years living in 118 hotels, playing to vast crowds in 147 concerts, surrounded at all times by security, requires a specific mindset, a shift out of 'normal' life. Everything is laid on. Every day is programmed in the tour 'bible' – even the days off see activities organized by the TAC, the Tour Activities Club, with more often than not a communal dinner on the evenings when there is no show.

> 'The thing about touring is that you are made to feel very important, but also treated as if you are seven years old.'
>
> Nick Mason of Pink Floyd

The current Stones touring operation is designed to give them the room they need to retain their own individuality and maintain normal working relationships. Security head Jim Callaghan has the attitude, 'You've just got to let them have their space.' Within the two or more floors of any hotel on which the band have descended, the four Stones have their own discreet, and discrete, suites with personal assistants and minders – Keith Richards has a gentleman helper, a kind of rock 'n' roll valet – and a distinctly personal environment.

Charlie Watts will spend his time sketching every hotel room, or shopping. Mick Jagger will be surfing the net, organizing his schedule, holding meetings. Keith Richards listens to music, always questing for fresh influence, new sounds. Ronnie Wood relaxes by holding an open house.

In the same way, their dressing rooms are set up and styled in a consistent fashion at every venue they play in, providing a regular, familiar personal space for each member of the band. Each dressing room reflects that band member's individual personality and provides some clues to the differences that fuel their creativity. Keith's room, dubbed 'Camp X-Ray', has a life-size cardboard cutout of Elvis with a joint dangling from his lips. Charlie Watts' space reflects his love of jazz and is aptly named 'The Cotton Club'. Mick is focused on fitness, the secret to the miles he runs on stage each night: his dressing room is called 'Work Out'. Ronnie's, styled for comfort, is known as 'Recovery'.

Alan Dunn, who has been in charge of tour logistics for over forty years, recalls that on the *Bigger Bang* tour, when the band played Wembley Stadium, they had so many different dressing-room requirements that the 'backstage area' was in fact the whole of Wembley Arena, itself normally a 12,500-seater venue . . .

The attitude of outsiders has also changed over the years. Jim Callaghan, as head of tour security, has observed the shift. 'It used to be "Look at that scum"; now the band are being entertained by Vice Presidents and dignitaries. And the police: one minute they're busting us and the next they're escorting us.'

Around the band the rest of the tour personnel find their own role. Long-time backing singer Lisa Fischer notes, 'There's a comfort, a security without there being a boredom. There's a lot of love, a lot of growth, a lot of allowing people to be who they are. Once you figure out where you fit in and what your role is, folks kind of know how to get you to do what they want you to do . . . We know the boundaries.' Outsiders must tread warily. When Ronnie Wood took a life coach on one tour, Keith identified an interloper in their midst – 'I can smell a fuckin' counsellor . . .'

The hierarchy within the touring party has been compared to the royal progress of a travelling medieval court. Opulence travels with them, with lavish furnishings and delicious food for all. But the rules – Lisa Fischer's boundaries – must be strictly observed. Alan Dunn tells new tour party members to be careful not to step over the invisible barrier. 'There is a fine line you can go up to. I tell new people, "Don't cross that line. Don't become a friend. Stay an employee. If you cross it, you are finished."'.

One of the most important of the unwritten rules concerns Keith Richards' specially prepared shepherd's pie, served before each show along with HP sauce, which must be imported from the UK, no other will do. Only Keith can take the first portion of shepherd's pie. Otherwise, all hell breaks loose. The rule is simple, but inviolable: 'Don't bust the crust!'

Beyond fighting the temptation to dive into Keith's pie, the primary skill of their core coterie of fifty to sixty people and the wider entourage – some 300 or more individuals ('The amount of people travelling with us, oh God,' in Charlie Watts' words) – is to ensure that by show time not only is all the huge interlinking of technical elements of staging, lighting, sound, props, backstage area, catering and dressing rooms in place, but that the four principals are ready to leave their bubbles and merge in their own way and in their own time to recreate the Rolling Stones as their fans expect them to be, and have paid for them to be.

Promoter Michael Cohl understands what the deal is. 'Even when they are not getting along, they get on stage and the magic clicks. It used to be more chaotic, more tension, people had a whole different attitude about it. People now are much more relaxed, much more professional.'

Life on tour is characterized by more than the big performances. The Stones submit themselves to a rigorous schedule of media interviews, 'meet and greets'. The one-time lengthy queues of star-struck hopeful groupies are now equally long lines of star-struck corporate execs and local dignitaries, although a handshake and a photo on the mobile phone is the only degree of starfucking the latter expect. Indeed, despite both Ronnie and Keith referring to looking forward to being on stage to get away from it all, the Stones all understand and are committed to the discipline of the tour. There is a deep sense of professionalism, an acknowledgement that the business end is what enables their passion for music.

Backstage before the show, Ronnie and Keith might spend

time together playing pool or snooker or grabbing a couple of acoustic guitars and jamming together on some old R&B numbers, while Charlie urbanely strolls around chatting to guests. Mick disappears early to prepare, running through some vocal exercises with band sideman Blondie Chaplin, loosening up in advance. These rituals are in place to provide a regular pattern that establishes a level of stability without becoming formulaic, that provides a sense of consistency from show to show without removing the leeway for improvisation and a special performance.

> 'When they walk on stage, they're not just musicians, they carry a lot of history with them. They always play great, but some nights they are brilliant.'
>
> Tony King, Rolling Stones PR

As much as the Rolling Stones and the teams surrounding them have prepared, the intensity goes up, 'past 11', when they get on stage in front of an audience. Nick Mason of Pink Floyd notes that even after six weeks of hard rehearsals, he would still get blisters from playing the first night. 'It could be six people or sixty thousand: the buzz from the audience, the excitement and challenge of playing for people is what it's all about.'

As in all families, much takes place without anybody saying anything. Keith states that he knows exactly what's happening simply by watching Charlie's left hand. If the tempo ever drags, one look to Keith from Ronnie speaks volumes. Both then glance at Charlie so he understands as well. Together they will then step up the pace. Everyone has mastered this silent language across years of practice, building familiarity into a common way of thinking. This telepathic communication is shared with all the regular sidemen: Chuck Leavell, bassist Darryl Jones, sax player Bobby Keyes and the three backing singers, Bernard Fowler, Lisa Fischer and Blondie Chaplin. The band perform as a unit, each individual listening and responding to the others in what Ronnie Wood calls 'a conversation through music'.

On Copacabana beach

The Copacabana concert was more complex than all the other 146 performances on the *Bigger Bang* tour. Above all, it was free, made possible through corporate sponsorship from two telecommunication companies and with Rio de Janeiro's municipal government bearing some of the infrastructure costs.

That it was taking place on a beach required a very specific set-up. The usual stage set was too heavy for the sand and the expected audience numbers necessitated screens and speakers to be set up along a mile and a half of the beach.

From the moment Mick Jagger won the crowd over by announcing 'Good evening, gang' in pitch-perfect Portuguese, to the grand finale of 'Satisfaction', the band and the tour team drew on all their experience going back over the previous forty-plus years, the concentration on hard work that typifies every superteam. As Keith later recalled, 'When I looked at the video of that show, I realized I was concentrating like a motherfucker. I mean grim! What had to be right was the sound, pal; didn't matter about the rest.'

TEAM TALK Building cohesion

Together for fifty years as a band, the Rolling Stones have played in more places to more people than any other band. An achievement all the more remarkable considering their very public long walk on the wild side. Mick Jagger agrees: 'Surviving with most of our fingers intact is our greatest achievement'.

Team cohesion is defined as a dynamic process that is reflected in the tendency of a group to remain united in the pursuit of its goals and objectives. It is the invisible force that keeps the team together and is the basis for high performance as a unit. The Stones offer many insights into the secret life of superteams and provide a number of lessons for all teams in how to build, maintain and rebuild cohesion.

In the beginning there was music. It provided the spark when Keith and Mick met on the station platform in Dartford and pulled the band together. The band's shared fascination with blues and rock 'n' roll was a common driving force in forming the band.

Early cohesion came from spending a lot of time together. The band lived, played and went everywhere together, piled into the back of a van along with their kit. They got to know each other intimately. Shared experiences and especially their early success helped reinforce the team's gelling together. In their initial guise as outlaws there was also a sense of the Stones united against the world, further strengthening their sense of belonging.

Harmonizing is about emphasizing differences together. From the outset, the Stones' music married lead, rhythm and bass guitars, drums, harmonica and Jagger's vocals. Cohesion also grew based on the team's recognition that each member of the band was a master of his own instrument or voice. They respect each other's capabilities. On stage they listen to each other intensely, playing off one another to release an energy greater than any could achieve individually or in parallel. The Stones' alchemy also represented a fusion of different personalities and passions.

The dynamic between Mick and Keith is the group's musical engine. They are the songwriting duo whose fraternal rivalry, reactions and combustions propel the group forward. The Stones' creativity on record and on stage is the result of a collision of their distinctive natures.

The combination of these combustible elements is also, however, inherently unstable. The seeds of the band's creativity, and in particular the dynamic between Keith and Mick, were also seeds that drove the band apart. Over the years this conflict has pushed the team close to breaking point. The challenge for the Stones – similar to many other teams – is in containing and channelling the fission, to build cohesion and keep the team together.

Bands find it hard to stay together. The challenge of several artists trying to paint on the same canvas at the same time is often too much to sustain. Failure tends to fragment, with blame always heaped on to the other band members: the singer had no charisma, the drummer couldn't keep time, the guitar player became a junkie, the bass player's wife didn't like his girl-friend, the manager stole the money . . . Most significantly, and despite being a cliché, musical differences do drive teams apart.

Long tours push members together with a mixture of intensity and boredom. The personal idiosyncrasies that were charming in the early days can become ceaselessly grating over time. The impact of success can provide a centrifugal force. A successful band living in a bubble where every whim is catered for by surrounding acolytes and adoring sycophants will send egos spinning outward into an individual rather than collect-ive focus.

Individual strengths are amplified through the team and unfortunately so are the dysfunctions. Mick Jagger's strong need to control and to be in charge was not always conducive to team-building, and even resulted in awakening Charlie Watts' fists of fury. While others in the band dabbled, the drug habits of Keith and Ronnie stretched the team's trust in each other to breaking point. It was less about the £20 million Ronnie is believed to have spent on drugs, or any moral judgement, rather the negative impact on their joint work which breached that trust. Not knowing when band members would turn up to write, rehearse or record put a strain on team cohesion. In true rock'n'roll terms it was not just drugs but sex and the changing flow of girlfriends and wives, with Charlie the notable exception, that challenged the team's togetherness.

Staying together by staying focused

The drivers that have kept the Stones together are applicable far beyond rock'n'roll. Maintaining and reinforcing cohesion is one of the central challenges in developing better teams. First and foremost, all the current Stones continue to be strongly committed to the goal of being the greatest rock'n'roll band in the world. No other band or project has come close in enabling the band members to fulfil their own personal ambitions. In terms of delivering fame, money and the chance to play for so many people or even all of the above, no other activity pursued in the various side projects has been as successful. Being a member of the Rolling Stones team continues to be the best way of achieving each individual's goals.

> 'I've never tried to achieve anything.
> I achieved everything I wanted to by being
> in the Rolling Stones and making records.
> That was the only real goal in life ever.'
> Keith Richards

Cohesion to a common purpose can help a team endure even the most difficult social tensions. Famously, Fleetwood Mac recorded their album *Rumours* as the band went through the sadness of break-ups and divorce. Vocalist Christine McVie and her ex-husband John, the band's bass player, had stopped talking completely except over musical matters. The relationship between the band's other feuding couple, guitarist Lindsey Buckingham and vocalist Stevie Nicks, was so tempestuous that they only stopped arguing to write music. Even Mick Fleetwood, the drummer, was in turmoil, having discovered that his wife was having an affair with his best friend. Only their shared commitment to making music – like Mick and Keith – was central to their creativity. They made their best work in the midst of their most difficult time together.

The Rolling Stones' lasting cohesion demonstrates the enduring power of assembling the right team. Each member is talented in his own role, and those roles are both distinct and complementary. In certain areas there is also a good fit in terms of personalities. Mick exercises control over many aspects of the band's life, but mainly in areas where the others have less interest in taking charge. Keith, Ronnie and Charlie are more focused on the music than on the business.

The creative abrasion between Keith and Mick is kept in balance by the solid straightforward nature of Charlie Watts and the mediating instincts and diplomatic approach of Ronnie Wood.

The band has also, over the years, developed cohesion by adopting a method of decision-making that works for them. In many instances Mick can take the lead, taking input from the others and with Keith effectively having veto rights. Keith reacts by exception, as when he rejected explosively the sweetcorn-themed stage designs proposed by the artist Jeff Koons ('fucking corn'). 'You know when Keith disagrees,' notes Ronnie Wood. 'He normally pulls a knife on you.'

Cohesion also comes from the team's wisdom in hiring a highly skilled supporting cast in all key areas of their operation to protect and enhance their own capabilities. The Stones are surrounded by a team who are trustworthy in terms of their competence, their reliability and their ability to fit in and around the four principals. For forty years, Prince Rupert Loewenstein was a perfect foil for Jagger on the business front, with his banker's eye and his appetite for deals and ever-improving business models. The Stones' partners need to be strong enough to be good partners and savvy and confident enough to know when and how to step back.

The Stones also build cohesion by maintaining some distance from each other. On tour their separate space is important, giving them their own personal areas when needed. The same is true with other personal projects, such as Mick Jagger's film production ventures and Ronnie's art. As long as these activities can be in parallel, seen as being 'as well as' and not 'instead of', they act as useful pressure-releasing valves. Indeed, performing outside the band enables them to appreciate the power of the team, since none of their individual ventures has ever been as successful as their joint one.

Allowing members to explore beyond its boundaries can strengthen the team: such activity is similar to a holiday, a bit of team tourism. Teams use opportunities such as coming back together after a break to give members the chance to recommit to the shared cause.

Much of the Stones' enduring success comes from mixing the traditional and the new. They rely on certain standards but also understand the need to keep things fresh. Changing the set list through the tour, weaving variations within each song, the band also feeds off the different energy from each new audience. The team can stay cohesive as long as they keep being interested and stimulated, as long as they keep growing.

In team environments, one of the toxic and divisive aspects can be the perception of unfairness or of being mistreated. A perceived lack of recognition or credit as well as uneven financial rewards, media interest and adulation can all pull a team apart. While the exact deal terms are kept a closely guarded secret, Keith and Mick share a far greater amount of the revenue, given their songwriting royalties. Even though the Stones are therefore unlikely to share equal rewards, there is a perceived fairness, which matters more than the absolute or even the relative amounts in maintaining cohesion.

The inherent instability of rock bands is a fact of life in the music industry. Few bands are successful; most flounder and then disband. Success brings its own challenges to keeping the team together. The Rolling Stones have mastered building and rebuilding team cohesion.

Forming, storming, norming, performing – and re-forming

Group dynamics theorist Bruce Tuckman's model of team development states that teams go through four stages in becoming effective. First is *forming*, where the members join the team and objectives are shared. Second is *storming*, in which the initial excitement and hope give way to differences in opinion and approach, leading to conflict. The third stage is *norming*, where the team discovers ways of resolving conflict and of working together. This leads to the final stage: *performing*, when the team has become effective at working as a unit.

The story of the Stones suggests that the best teams go back and forth over these stages again and again. They are able to form and re-form, as needed, bringing in new talent to help maintain the high standards and add new ideas. They also take breaks and consciously choose to re-form and recommit to the common purpose and each other.

The core of the Stones' success is the energy generated by the creative abrasion amongst the team members. Storming has provided an important edge in keeping the Stones vibrant. The Stones' determination to put consistent effort into rehearsals and the disciplined routines they employ in preparing for their concerts are examples of norming activity that is revisited on an ongoing basis to ensure the team performs consistently. As with the SAS and their constant training of teamwork, the Stones show that teamwork does not come easy.

A danger of the norming phase is that teams become so cohesive and comfortable with each other and their approach that their creative edge is dulled. To avoid this, Pixar even developed protocols to ensure that they continued to storm in order to deliver the creativity they knew their films needed. For the Rolling Stones, the storming seems built-in, especially between Jagger and Richards. Part of their longevity and staying power comes from having developed norms or protocols to deal with the recurring storms, harmonizing the diverse skills but not averaging them.

The Rolling Stones keep going together because they can, and because they still want to. As long as the fans want to see them perform, the Stones will keep playing. The buzz of performance is the ultimate, and only, satisfaction – and they still want every concert to be better than the last one.

AGENDA Build cohesion

Cohesion is the magnetic force that binds a team together and enables it to perform effectively as a unit. Two powerful ways of building cohesion are by forging a clear and compelling team purpose and ensuring your team is well led. A further factor in getting your team to stick together is the trust and commitment that develops between teammates. Teams need time to gel and trust can take time to build, but there are a host of ways for you and your team to accelerate team cohesion.

Earn trust through competence. Give team members the chance to show off their skills. Team members earn trust when they can demonstrate that they are masters of their task and prove their competence to contribute to the team's purpose. You can turbocharge trust-building by focusing on quick wins that build your teammates' trust in each other's capabilities.

Earn trust through reliability. Team members earn trust when they do what they say they will do. That can be as simple as turning up on time. When team members deliver on their promises and demonstrate reliability, they earn your trust. Your ability to remain consistent and reliable under pressure and through testing times will have the biggest determinant of how much your team trusts you.

Earn trust by showing you care. Trust within the team grows when members feel that they are being heard and understood, when their views are respected even if not agreed with. You can earn trust by demonstrating that you have your teammates' best interests at heart. Backing them up when they need extra help, going the extra mile to support them and showing your appreciation for their efforts are all trust-building behaviours, especially if done equally across the team rather than only with a favoured few.

Earn trust by trusting. Trust is reciprocal: trusting your teammates is a powerful way of earning their trust. Being able to be vulnerable in front of teammates, admitting mistakes or asking for help can make it much easier for others to follow your lead and create a climate of openness.

Earn trust by spending quality time together. We trust people we know well. Getting to know each other as people and looking for simple human common ground is a tried-and-tested route to team-building. Looking each other in the eye, the intimacy of genuine human contact, breaking bread together – these are age-old and enduringly powerful ways of bringing people closer. Having fun together needs to be natural: you cannot force it, but you can create the conditions where you can all relax and enjoy each other's company. A feature of global business is how dispersed some teams are. Such 'virtual' teams require the same tasks for building and developing as any other team. You still need to forge common purpose, select the 'best people', not the 'people who are best', create conditions for success and manage the team dynamics. If anything, the challenge of building trust between the team members is greater. Personal contact remains vital as a basis for cohesion and can be reinforced – but not replaced – by social media and digital connectivity.

Earn trust by overcoming conflict and crisis. Surviving the inevitable conflict accelerates trust in a team. 'Storming together' is a key step in becoming an effective team, but facing a crisis that occurs before trust is firmly established can cause terminal damage to your team. You should invest early in building cohesion as trust tends to be scarce when you need it the most. Creating a reservoir of goodwill will help cushion the blows from creative conflict and allow your team to stay connected through strong disagreements.

'Dialogue is crucial to any effort
to find a solution to conflict.'

Gerry Adams

6
THE NORTHERN IRELAND PEACE PROCESS
Courage and choreography

Good Friday, 10 April 1998,
Stormont, Belfast, Northern Ireland

Just under one year after Tony Blair has come to power as British Prime Minister, he is within touching distance of a celebrated triumph: an accord between the bitterly divided factions within Northern Ireland. To reach this point he has orchestrated a team composed of implacable enemies who, initially, will not even talk together face to face. With the courageous help of many parties, notably Irish Taoiseach Bertie Ahern, the parties involved have inched forward, painfully and painstakingly, towards an agreement.

Tony Blair had been Prime Minister for only eleven days when he told Alastair Campbell, his communications director and one of his closest advisers, that he could see a way forward on Northern Ireland. His optimistic remarks to Campbell on

12 May 1997 were classic Blair, spoken as if he was the first and possibly the only person who could make it happen.

Four days later he was delivering a carefully crafted speech at the Royal Ulster Agricultural Show. He took a strong unionist stance ('I believe in the United Kingdom. I value the Union'), but also opened the way for government officials to restart talks with Sinn Féin, and finally underlined the power and the importance of consent. The fundamental principle was that a political democratic process, rather than violence, was the only acceptable way forward. His comments that day were no empty sound bites, as the Good Friday Agreement proved.

That Agreement marked a hugely significant moment in Northern Ireland's history, the culmination of a sustained period of determined team-building, bringing together sworn enemies against a backdrop of decades of violence, atrocities and failed peace efforts. The stakes were huge and the team dynamics involved were fraught, fragile and volatile.

The very name of the Agreement, signed on that Easter weekend of 1998, highlights the difficulties that were inherent in bringing this particular team together. The unionists called it the Belfast Agreement, the nationalists the Good Friday Agreement. Even at the point of agreement, they could not settle on a name.

All the machinations and negotiations that had preceded the Good Friday Agreement of April 1998 were merely the opening act. A further nine years of far from smooth progress – a journey full of false hopes, threatened collapses, allegations and counter-allegations, suspicions and suspensions, but at least sustained momentum – would be required before the formation of a new Northern Ireland Executive in May 2007 marked the completion of the peace process. The signing of the Good Friday Agreement was an essential step in the journey to peace. It demonstrated that progress was possible and laid the foundations for the teamwork needed over the next nine years to achieve a lasting resolution.

Tony Blair's vision of peace for Northern Ireland had started against the backdrop of a dauntingly huge chasm between the future team members. Wise heads in the Civil Service, former ministers, and seasoned journalists who had covered the Troubles in Northern Ireland since the late 1960s, all told him that there was far too much history to overturn: the 3,600 deaths, too many long-held memories of revenge, a whole lore of bitter resentments. The weight of history was potentially suffocating.

Winston Churchill, in the immediate aftermath of the First World War, had remarked of the division between Northern Ireland's unionists and nationalists, 'The integrity of their quarrel is one of the few institutions that has been unaltered in the cataclysm which has swept the world.'

Yet against this lengthy history, and within this complex, multifaceted situation, Tony Blair saw an opportunity for peace. He recognized that with Labour's election to power there was a brief window of opportunity for action while he held a commanding Commons majority. Above all, Tony Blair and his core advisers came to proceedings with considerably less baggage than their predecessors, although if required some potentially relevant baggage could always be found – Blair and his Chief of Staff Jonathan Powell both had Irish antecedents. Tony Blair's grandfather had been an Orangeman, though Blair himself had converted to Catholicism after marrying Cherie. He was consequently informed by one leading Orange Order member that he had therefore 'sold his birthright'.

The way forward required intensely delicate choreography. Each member of the peace process team had to be guided on to a parallel path of positive movement. Often this was a question of symbolic gesture rather than substance, but the gesture in itself represented a degree of movement. Sustaining momentum was the route to momentous change. Maintaining the pace of the talks was critical. As Jonathan Powell said, 'We did not have a detailed, worked-out, point-by-point strategy, but we did have an idea. We would take events at a gallop.'

In fact, although there was no predefined strategy, Blair re-energized the process around the all-powerful idea of peace. A valuable, historic prize. The focus on the outcome was clear to everyone, and if the path to attain it was going to be always meandering, often rocky and frequently treacherous, the goal served the purpose of completely focusing all parties concerned, whatever their own particular starting point.

To maintain momentum towards that goal, Blair and his advisers applied – whether wittingly or not – a process that delivered progress through three phases. It is a process that has since been presented as a framework for the resolution of protracted conflicts.

Initially they set out to neutralize the fears and the paranoia of all parties, fears that each constituency firmly believed to be completely legitimate. If those fears could be mitigated the momentum could be maintained. If not, obsession with past conflict and disagreements would prevent a clear view of a possible, different future.

Building on that neutralizing of fears, the second phase was to humanize the process and the people involved. For both sides their opponents were cast as bogeymen, the protagonists demonized, stereotyped, even silenced: the previous Conservative government had sunk to the level of banning TV and radio stations from broadcasting the actual voices of the Sinn Féin leaders – actors were hired to speak their words. Through human dialogue and often banal niceties, they began to see each other as human beings, even to share a joke.

The third phase grew organically from there. Only with the other two phases in place could everyone move on to harmonize. Only then could opposing parties talk about common goals and begin to transition from enemies into a functioning team.

The process was paramount. The goal – peace – was all-powerful. The skill was to stay in the process at all times. If the momentum ever wavered, the process itself had to be maintained. At many stages, that consisted of holding meetings simply to discuss a timetable and the protocol for organizing subsequent meetings. The process and the negotiations ground on slowly, but as long as it ground forward, there was still hope.

When Sinn Féin's Martin McGuinness and Ken Maginnis

of the Ulster Unionist Party (UUP) held a public debate, 'it wasn't a great debate', noted Gerry Adams in his memoirs. 'Maginnis was not on good form. Its significance was that it had happened at all.' Significance and symbolism had to come first, before substance. Perceptions had to be changed before practice. Together they formed a Giant's Causeway of stepping stones to success.

By intricately plotting that sequence of small steps everybody could move, albeit frustratingly slowly, in the same direction.

> 'We had to keep things moving forward, like a bicycle. If we ever let the bicycle fall over, we would create a vacuum and that vacuum would be filled by violence.'
>
> Jonathan Powell

Neutralizing the risks and the fears

The key players on both sides – the nationalists and the unionists, whether extremist or moderate – had to perform an extraordinarily difficult balancing act. They were being asked by Tony Blair to achieve a deal under the strain of a schizophrenic existence as, simultaneously, enemies and peacemakers.

If they were too aggressive, truculent or stubborn, the neutral observer would doubt their genuine commitment to the peace process. If, however, they seemed to be leaning too much towards making concessions, their own core community or constituency would question their leadership. This led to constant toing and froing as leaders would agree a detail in principle but then have to go back to their colleagues who might immediately veto the decision.

Ultimately the UUP leader David Trimble was unable to reconcile these two demands. Despite the appreciation of the others in the team (Northern Ireland Secretary Mo Mowlam admired his 'impressive' iron will), and the recognition of the Nobel Peace Prize, he sacrificed himself in 2002, and 'took one for the team' to allow things to move on.

It was the same delicate balance for all the politicians. Mo Mowlam, whose role was vital in the early stages because she was able to reach out to the nationalists, was therefore inevitably seen by the unionists as far too sympathetic towards the nationalist cause. The degrees of latitude were slender. Thus the neutralization was a lengthy phase, as any sudden movements could endanger any lessening of fears.

Some of this neutralization was achieved through a subtle blend of covert and overt discussions. Talks between the Sinn Féin politicians and the IRA High Command had to be held in complete secrecy, Martin McGuinness and Gerry Adams being shuttled to isolated barns in the back of sheep trucks, or sitting in the spare rooms of sympathizers' houses in the suburbs of Belfast. 'Back channel' dialogue had also been ongoing, albeit intermittently, between the British government and the IRA via MI6 and with the aid of some helpful intermediaries, from the 1970s onwards.

The use of these back channel routes achieved a degree of neutralization by virtue of the fact that they were much less scary if no one knew the discussions were happening.

In contrast, the public talks at Stormont took place under the full spotlight of media attention. Every move, every arrival or departure, was observed by the news teams camped outside. Every statement, prepared or off the cuff, was analysed incessantly. Each action contained the potential to derail the entire process. One ill-judged word, careless comment or misguided gesture and the two sides would jolt atavistically back to their long-held positions, allowing fear and mistrust to cloud their view once more. Or one moment of violence – like the Omagh bombing of 1998 – could threaten to reverse any recent progress.

That the discussions were happening in the heart of Belfast was telling – the parties had not decamped to a neutral venue. Belfast was hugely territorial, lamp posts and kerbstones marking the sectarian borders. The city was still rife with danger: in early 1998 the husband of one of Gerry Adams' nieces was murdered. But perhaps the setting helped force the issue, normalizing proceedings as the city carried on its regular daily existence. As Gerry Adams put it: 'All around us – skirting the pandemonium, the killing, the dying – buses and cars whizzed by, people got on with their lives.'

The Castle Buildings annex at Stormont chosen as the venue for the Good Friday negotiations was far from ideal. Adams thought it reeked of 'a Boer mentality', Blair that it was ugly, cramped and had no soul. It was an unremarkable sixties building full of anonymous, identical rooms, narrow corridors, with no useful nooks and crannies for private chinwags. Hillsborough Castle, the residence of the Secretary of State for Northern Ireland was far prettier but gave off a strong whiff of old colonialism with its manicured green lawns and the portraits of former monarchs, which would have sent completely the wrong message to the nationalists. In Castle Buildings at least no one had favoured status, and in that sense it was the perfect place to negotiate for peace.

The location of conversations anywhere was always loaded with significance. The urbane setting, paintings and antiques in the Foreign and Commonwealth Office's Lancaster House represented, from a republican point of view, the cultural theft of an imperialist power. When the Sinn Féin leadership arrived at No. 10 Downing Street and Martin McGuinness remarked, 'So this is where the damage was done,' the Brits immediately assumed he was referring to the 1991 IRA mortar attack – McGuinness was thinking of the 1921 Anglo-Irish Treaty signed there by Michael Collins, which had allowed Northern Ireland the option to break away from the Irish Free State . . .

It was at Castle Buildings that Blair met US Senator George Mitchell and Canadian General John de Chastelain, brought in to chair the body overseeing decommissioning, who informed him that they estimated the chances of reaching agreement to be less than 20 per cent. It prompted Blair to take full charge of the process, setting up temporary offices and plunging himself into the thick of the negotiation, including the drafting and the consideration of a long menu of details, among them the subtleties of seating arrangements.

At early meetings in 1997 and 1998, to avoid arguments all the parties present were seated in alphabetical order. As the reality of power-sharing grew closer in 2007, even the physical shape of furniture was of critical importance. The table that the Northern Ireland Executive would use became a significant issue. The Democratic Unionists wanted the two parties to sit across from each other, as adversaries. Sinn Féin, on the other hand, wanted Ian Paisley to be sitting next to Gerry Adams – sharing power. It was a British civil servant, Robert Hannigan, who came up with the idea of using a diamond-shaped table which allowed Paisley and Adams to be seated on either side of one of its apexes – 'thereby being both opposite each other and next to each other'.

Humanizing the demons

The extent of the personal divide between the two sides was made starkly evident when the Ulster Unionist Ken Maginnis was invited to talk to Sinn Féin and angrily declared, 'I don't talk to fucking murderers.'

To counter those attitudes, Bill Clinton, offering support to the process as President of the United States, would cite a line from one of his predecessors John F. Kennedy: 'Civility is not a sign of weakness.' Jonathan Powell expressed a similar sentiment: 'I think it is always right to talk to your enemy, however badly they are behaving.'

During a visit to America in the Thatcher years, Gerry Adams had appeared on the *Larry King Show* with Maginnis. Michael Mates, a government minister, was also in the US and appeared on television with Adams, who pointed out that neither Maginnis nor Mates would deign to speak to him in the UK, but were perfectly prepared to fly across the Atlantic to do so. On *Larry King*, Adams offered Maginnis his hand. Maginnis refused to take it, and that one negative gesture went down badly with the American viewers.

At an early meeting between the parties in the peace process, Tony Blair made a point of going around shaking hands with everyone. It was a simple symbol of human connection. 'No one received a shock,' observed Gerry Adams wryly.

Politesse obliges that human, humane connection, just as diplomatic protocol and etiquette have always been a way of defusing tension by concentrating on detail. The mundane removes risk. During the mid-1970s Gerry Adams remembered meeting two former Presbyterian moderators 'over tea and scones in the parlour of Councillor Marie Moore's home. By such niceties are barriers broken down.'

One of Tony Blair's core skills was his ability to understand the importance of the gesture, and to understand how it would play out in public. His impromptu speech on the morning after Princess Diana's death was a classic example of this. He was able to put himself in others' shoes – yet while seeing things from their point of view, he kept his eyes steadfastly on the prize. That made him a powerful persuader.

Mo Mowlam brought a degree of cheerful panache to proceedings. She blithely ignored the huffing and puffing of the bluffly male politicians, and although she often felt sidelined by Tony Blair's kitchen cabinet, she played an instrumental role.

Vitally, her very presence sent out a message to the republican and nationalist side that the new British government was a very different beast from the previous Thatcher and Major administrations. She specifically noted in her autobiography that she had tried to humanize the situation, inviting Elton John to play at the first of a series of annual concerts in Northern Ireland. Ian Paisley characteristically retorted, 'Now she's bringing sodomites to Stormont.'

She trusted her instincts, as when – against the advice of No. 10 – she flew to meet prisoners in the Maze after the unionist Billy Wright had been killed there by nationalist prisoners as part of one of the endless tit-for-tat murders. 'It is very important that everyone is given dignity if you expect them to take you seriously,' she remarked. 'By the very act of visiting these men they knew that I was taking them seriously.' And again, the significance outweighed the content. 'It was really of very little importance what was said.'

'She was instinctively right and we were wrong,' admitted Jonathan Powell. 'There is no way it would have been possible for us to reach agreement on Good Friday 1998 if Mo had not breached the barrier with her ebullient personality.'

Gerry Adams 'liked her style. Sometimes she was provocative. Other times, she was funny.' On the eve of the Good Friday Agreement she worked the fringes, keeping conversations and that all-important dialogue going.

Bill Clinton also helped to humanize the process. He was willing to be, wanted to be, everybody's friend. He provided an external but intimate level of common ground. Clinton was an active bringer together and energizer. Despite his own problems at home on both the political and domestic fronts (1998 was the year of the Monica Lewinsky scandal) he made himself available at key moments and would phone up in the middle of his night to prompt, advise, cajole. He understood that continuing the conversation was key.

Equally important was Bertie Ahern, the Republic of Ireland Taoiseach. He was 'a natural conciliator', but 'tough and shrewd' according to Gerry Adams. Ahern, who had been a negotiator with trade unions and understood the way to negotiate, brought common sense and practicality to the process. He showed he was prepared to make personal sacrifices by flying back in for important talks direct from his own mother's vigil.

Humour and humanity

Although the issues at the heart of the discussions were hugely serious, and genuinely a matter of life and death, what emerges is that there was also a capacity for humour, albeit gallows humour at times, and the key participants, however sternly committed to their own cause, were able to step back at critical moments.

At the start of the four-day and four-night session in the Castle Buildings leading up to the 1998 agreement, Alastair Campbell recognized that the Prime Minister was nervous when Blair put on a thick Irish accent and pretended to be a newsreader announcing that, as part of the deal for peace, Cherie would convert to Protestantism and that he was going to speak like an Irishman. In breaks from the talks in the offices that he called his 'cell', he went with Campbell to get some air in a small garden, referring to it as prison exercise. Bertie Ahern was only half joking when he said that if he had too much exposure to the UUP hardline deputies Ken Maginnis and John Taylor he might end up thumping them. Black humour was a vital part of the coping mechanism for the participants. Under huge pressure to make a historic agreement to achieve a lasting peace, the jokes were a welcome if only momentary release.

There is a famous photograph of Tony Blair, Bertie Ahern, Ian Paisley and Martin McGuinness sitting in Stormont shortly after the final power-sharing agreement was signed – Ian Paisley has just told a joke and everyone is laughing. It does not look forced. Paisley, by all accounts, was a completely different, gregarious soul in private, in direct contrast to his fulminating public persona.

Gerry Adams tells a story that in the evening after the Agreement had been signed he nipped outside in the grounds of Stormont to take a leak. He came across a leading unionist who had had the same idea. Adams turned and said, 'This is the pee process.' The unionist 'had the grace to smile'. From such small human contacts is progress made.

A final harmony

> 'Forgiving is not forgetting. It is actually
> remembering – remembering and
> not using your right to hit back.'
> Archbishop Desmond Tutu

At this point, the difficult issues could finally be addressed. All the previous work to knit the team together was vital because in the end the resolution had to be from harmony between the furthest extremes, not harmony at the moderate centre. Only if the IRA – whose High Command were the invisible presence during all the talks – as represented by Sinn Féin, and the far reaches of unionism in the form of Ian Paisley could find some kind of common ground would a final agreement work.

Ian Paisley, thinks Jonathan Powell, changed the dynamic of this later phase significantly after recovering from illness. He was reborn and committed to securing resolution as his legacy. 'He went from Mr No to Mr Yes,' says Powell.

Another line of thought is that even the extremists in the IRA and the unionist paramilitaries found themselves outflanked in extremism by the events of 9/11. Suddenly the outrages perpetrated by Al-Qaeda set a benchmark which the Irish paramilitaries would never consider. Their actions and activities seemed out of date; the world order had changed.

Above all, the peace process ultimately worked because of the bringing together of human beings. The original Good Friday Agreement would not have been possible without the leadership of Tony Blair, John Hume, David Trimble, Gerry Adams and Martin McGuinness, or Bertie Ahern and Bill Clinton. In time Ian Paisley would be needed and would step up too. The depth of conflict and the demands of the peace process necessitated that these team members were also big leaders at their best.

The Social Democratic and Labour Party leader John Hume had the vision and courage years ahead to begin to pull the IRA towards a political resolution. The UUP's David Trimble put peace before his own political career. Together, Hume and Trimble were rightly awarded the Nobel Peace Prize in 1998. Adams and McGuinness managed the transition from men of violence to respected politicians, risking their lives in doing so. David Ervine, the leader of the Progressive Unionist Party, was similarly brave in his denunciation of the violence he had once embraced and advocated.

The peace process was a journey, not an event, and at each step there were opportunities for the different members to either earn or destroy trust. Team-building is also a journey and opportunities to earn trust often come naturally from teamwork over time. Actual teamwork is the best environment for team members to demonstrate their competence, reliability and care for each other's interests. Equally, team-building based on similar opportunities for people to earn their teammates' trust can be powerful, especially when compared to abstract and frankly inane team-building games.

That element of trust was vital at critical moments throughout the peace process. On the morning of the Good Friday Agreement, Tony Blair's press adviser Alastair Campbell announced to the media that a deal had been done, but in fact not all the parties had seen the final text. When they did, the unionists threatened to pull out. David Trimble, the UUP leader, said things were now 'hopeless'.

The Blair team rushed to draft and agree one critical paragraph, tore it out of the printer and got the new wording signed off in the nick of time. Even after months and months of negotiation and the patient building of the peace process team, in the end success or failure came down to a few seconds of panic. Tony Blair's staff had forgotten to save the paragraph on their computer, though, so some weeks later the Northern Ireland Office had to politely and discreetly request a copy from the UUP, who had the only original. The trust held and the copy was, without fuss or recrimination, delivered: another small step along the road to – in retrospect – remarkable change.

A few weeks after the power-sharing executive had been set up in 2007, Jonathan Powell took a call from a civil servant, who reported that Ian Paisley was feeling tired as he had been up doing Scottish Irish dancing the night before with Martin McGuinness. 'It dawned on me,' said Powell, 'quite how much things had changed.'

TEAM TALK Mastering conflict

Tony Blair was the catalyst and key architect of peace in Northern Ireland. He was clear that resolving the conflict was not possible alone. He fundamentally understood from the outset that peace required the involvement and commitment of all members of the political parties in the north and south of Ireland and the United Kingdom, the support of the American administration and also his own core advisers. He recognized that to deliver peace he had to transform these enemies into an effective team.

Managing conflict and transforming it into better teamwork is a core superteam skill. The peace process demonstrates that engaging conflicting parties is not only possible but necessary to build the team.

Few teams will need to overcome an equivalent burden of hate and history of violence, but many can learn from the lessons that the Northern Ireland peace process offers on building trust and mastering conflict.

Creating common purpose was at the heart of the peace process. The deal was doable so long as it allowed both sides to declare victory – a real feat, given it was a zero-sum game. The Agreement could be seen to strengthen the union between the

United Kingdom and Northern Ireland and move decisively in the direction of a united Ireland at the same time. But the incompatibility of the two sides' definition of victory was the very reason for the conflict and created the need for the peace process, rather than ensuring it succeeded.

The process worked because there was a higher purpose than the cherished but irreconcilable objectives of unionists and nationalists. The process held at its core the importance of consent – that the will of the majority of the people of Ireland, north and south, should determine their future. As such, the common purpose of the team was focused on the means by which each side would pursue its own objectives, rather than the objectives themselves. The essence of the agreement was a shared commitment to a peaceful and democratic approach to achieving their conflicting political goals.

The common purpose of removing the gun from Irish politics and the commitment to peaceful means was central in creating the cohesion necessary for the enemies to work together. Cohesion and teamwork were vital since resolution required all members of the overall team to operate together as peaceful political parties, not terrorist organizations. Peace was possible only if all sides were party to a common agreement.

It was also important that the shared prize did not require either the unionists or the nationalists to abandon their own goals entirely. To ensure they could carry their constituents with them, all parties needed to promote and protect their own interests. The common purpose not only offered an objective that could be shared across the political parties but also allowed participants to continue to serve their deeply held interests.

The self-interests of the leaders who signed up to the Agreement were a mixture of the spiritual, the desire to represent and help their specific communities, and their desire to acquire political power. For the Northern Irish politicians like David Trimble it offered the chance to devolve power from Westminster, and for the already elected leaders such as Tony Blair it offered the electoral benefits of achieving peace where others had failed.

For all the leaders, the attraction of leaving a lasting legacy by being a peacemaker and bringing an end to the mounting list of casualties and families fractured by grief, to 'unlock the better side of humanity amongst their people', was a powerful motivator.

As well as harnessing the individual needs of the leaders, the peace process also needed to manage their fear of being branded traitors and the ensuing consequences. In the end it was David Trimble who paid the highest political price when the concessions he made to get the Agreement signed served as ammunition for Paisley to take over as the majority unionist leader.

The Northern Ireland peace process demonstrates the power of focusing on a common purpose that unites team members and taps into rather than supersedes individual self-interest. Emphasizing the downside risks of not playing the team game are also important levers in promoting collective action.

It also demonstrates two aspects of how common purpose helps master conflict. The more obvious is the focus on creating a win-win situation for both sides, the more important is managing the downside risks for all parties. The process had to neutralize the fears and concerns of the team members, as a critical step to moving forward.

Maintaining the momentum

Mechanisms to get people and keep people on the same team train are often necessary. There is no question that the speed and pace set by Tony Blair created a sense of urgency that mobilized action from all parties. By setting out a clear deadline and a timetable for action he created a momentum for that action. Over the following decade, the deadline became a much devalued currency but it was one of the few elements that pulled the divergent members of the process in the same direction.

Blair's recognition that peace is a process, not an event, was fundamental. The key was forward momentum, regardless of how slow and relentless it was, even in the face of violent attempts to derail the process. The process moved one step at a time and the members consolidated team-building and teamwork gains at each stage to make slipping back harder to do. In moving the train forward the team used intensely delicate choreography. Fundamental to the collaboration required for the peace process, Blair and his team were continuously balancing the needs of the different parties. Offers and concessions to either side needed to be matched to ensure that everyone inched forward together.

Most teams will not face such conflict between members. But the lessons of balancing the see-saw are still relevant. Ensuring all participants were treated fairly, or at least in ways they *perceived* were fair, was critical in Northern Ireland and can be applied to teams in general. In situations where all participants need to be involved and engaged, where no one can win if the team loses, a sense of fairness in the way team members are treated is essential to ensure that all of them give their fullest commitment and effort. Favouritism and special treatment drive a wedge between participants, breeding resentment and leading to mistrust.

At the heart of the Agreement were the Mitchell Principles: a set of six ground rules to which all parties agreed to adhere. They made explicit the acceptable and unacceptable norms of conduct for the participants and provided the fundamental basis for the more detailed agreement that was to follow. As described in other superteam stories, developing a set of clear, shared ideas that govern the team's interactions and behaviour is a powerful means for achieving effective collaboration and cohesion. For Northern Ireland the common purpose, the Principles and finally the detailed Heads of Agreement that followed from them, were fundamentally the same. The means reflected the common end. That is, the peaceful, legal and democratic notion of consent was both the higher goal and the mechanism for achieving it.

For other teams the protocols and principles defining team action do not need to be the same as the common purpose, but they should be aligned with it. Setting out in black and white what is acceptable behaviour and what is not helps shape team performance. In Northern Ireland the core principles shaping team behaviour were that violence was unacceptable, whereas democratic peaceful means were highly desirable.

The Heads of Agreement also outlined the focus of inter-action and negotiation. In situations of high pressure and high stakes, being explicit about how the team will interact, the choreography for collaboration, enables the team to have a shared understanding and limits risk. Agreeing the agenda for important meetings helps ensure individuals are prepared and focused on the right things, securing more effective col-laboration from the team.

Most importantly, the peace process that led to the Good Friday Agreement demonstrated that an accord was possible. It laid down the patterns and the practice for further nego-tiations. Peaceful means of achieving objectives, not allowing violence to derail the settlement train, were becoming more commonplace. The right location and architecture were also essential for collaboration. Certainly, the Castle Buildings in Belfast were far from ideal in an architectural perspective, but they were neutral and in that sense fit for purpose. Talking became the new normal, pursuing peace a habit.

Trusting the human instinct

Simple human contact and manners are a foundation for teams to engage in more meaningful dialogue, especially if they are starting from a point of conflict. Within all teams, it is difficult to achieve the teamwork or team-building necessary without dialogue between members. In Northern Ireland dialogue was first achieved indirectly, through the bilateral or trilateral 'proximity talks'. For trust to develop, face-to-face dialogue was essential.

Friendship was as much a feature of the process as hatred. The chemistry between Blair and Ahern, and between Blair and Clinton, created bonds that made their support of the process far stronger. Over the decade of the overall peace process a degree of friendship even emerged between the Sinn Féin leaders and Blair and his team. Friendship is positive but not vital. Gerry Adams points to Nelson Mandela's relationship with Frederik de Klerk, the last president of the apartheid era. According to Mandela, 'We get on well, but we do not hang out together very often.'

More important than friendship is a personal relationship between members that is based on mutual respect and empathy. Blair asked both sides to see the other's perspective. It was his own natural empathetic core skills which often helped move the process forward, keeping the team of enemies together. He was a master at understanding different counterparts' positions, both in terms of substance and in terms of emotions. This was a political skill, demonstrated too in his remarks following the death of Princess Diana. It was also a personal skill – in offering support and challenge to David Trimble and Gerry Adams, he could identify with and appreciate the challenges and risks that both men were taking.

Empathy requires team members to be able to listen and hear the content as well as the meaning of what their colleagues are saying. It means being able to see things through your teammates' eyes, to see and feel their perspective. As Tony Blair put it, 'If it matters to them, it matters to me.' It also requires that individual team members are able to demonstrate, whether in words or actions, that they have understood both the substance and the emotions expressed. Ensuring all team members are heard and understood is essential to building trust between them.

For trust to be earned, since it resides in the perceptions of others, the ability to be empathetic is vital, but it also requires demonstrating competence, the ability to deliver – whether through expert knowledge, skill, or power and influence. Reliability also earns trust, the sense that you will make good on your promises . . . every time. Finally, earning trust demands that you have the other person's best interests at heart. It is not how well and how long teammates know each other that matters, but how much they have earned each other's trust.

The peace process in Northern Ireland demonstrated the need for neutralizing fears, humanizing the parties as the basis for harmonizing the team and mastering conflict, and ultimately the ability to forgive, if not forget. The leaders in the Northern Ireland superteam had to be strong and stalwart representatives of their respective communities. In driving for the shared purpose of future peace and renouncing conflict, they also had to forgive the past and compromise for the common good.

AGENDA Master conflict

Too much friction between members can cause progress to grind to a halt. When energy is directed inwards, to internal team conflict, teams lose focus about their customers, their competitors and their core purpose. At its most divisive conflict is a centrifugal force that can fragment your team. Yet avoiding conflict altogether is not the answer. The ability to master conflict is a vital part of becoming a better team and delivering high performance.

Encourage creative abrasion. Contrary to the myth of the harmonious team, your goal is not to build a team without conflict, but to channel conflict effectively. You need to harness the energy and creativity that comes from the combination of push and pull between the diverse members of your team.

Guard against groupthink. Cohesion is not a one-way street in teams. There can be too much of a good thing. Be alert to the dangers of your team becoming too cohesive. In particular watch out for your team's desire for harmony and consensus overriding the need for robustly reviewing options in the search for the best answer. The conditions for group-think are the presence of a strong leader, a cohesive group and strong external pressures. All three characteristics are positive determinants of team success, but overplayed and unleavened by conflict they can push your team towards the dark side.

Neutralize fears. Fight or flight is the first instinctive response to any potential threat of loss. If faced with silence or violence between individual team members, consider what they might be afraid of. Don't forget that people are both rational and emotional – it could be an actual loss of power or a perceived loss of respect. When your team is set against itself and divided by internal conflict you have to defuse fears and reassure both sides before you can begin to move forward together.

Beware of the easy average answer. You will also need to be cautious about compromise. Of course when the costs of conflict are very high, such as in Northern Ireland, compromise is a better solution than the alternative of continuing violence. Splitting the difference has the merit of being a fast and fair resolution to conflict in your team, with both sides giving and getting something. If your team meets in the middle too often, however, you run the risk of ending up with average answers rather than the most creative ones where everyone wins.

Eyes on the prize. Clear and compelling common purpose ensures your team is committed and focuses on what really matters. Your objective should be to find a win-win-win solution, satisfying each side of the conflict and the team as a whole. Reminding your team about common purpose ensures a focus on your shared goal and the need to work together.

Don't sweat the small stuff. You can take a lead and avoid arguments over the petty and immaterial. Save your energy for the necessary vigorous discussions on the issues at the heart of your team's core purpose.

Keep things civil. The difference between a plan being branded 'ill-conceived' and a teammate being called 'stupid' is what separates teams that work from teams that don't. Conflict about ideas is productive and conflict that is personal is destructive. Like a boxing referee, you should remind your team to keep the fight clean.

Keep talking and, even better, keep listening. It is always better to have bitter arguments at the negotiating table than violence on the streets. To go further, take your cue from Mo Mowlam and balance how much you advocate your position with listening and inquiry, to better understand others' perspectives. The virtue of teamwork comes from the shared search for the truth. That means you need to actively encourage different opinions to be heard and understood, even if those opinions are uncomfortable and ones that you disagree with.

Be fair and share. To build cohesion and minimize conflict, you need to spread the love and share the pain as evenly as you can. Few things divide faster than a leader constantly favouring a subset of the team. This does not mean everything, including rewards, has to be equally divided but it needs to be perceived as fair. While everyone is entitled to his own opinion, you should also ensure the facts are shared. You can often settle difficult discussions much more quickly by letting the data speak for itself.

Seek commitment not consensus. Of course, complete consensus is powerful, but getting everyone to agree can take an age to achieve, if it can be achieved at all. To build commitment it can help if you clearly differentiate between discussion and decisions. You will find that most team members understand they cannot always have the final say or get their own way every time. You are much more likely to get your team to disagree yet still commit if they feel they have been heard and understood.

Forgive but not forget. It may need you to go first, taking the risk that others might not follow, but at the heart of mastering conflict is the courage you will need to forgive your teammates. Seeing the other side and their humanity, recognizing that they are not perfect and neither are you, is the basis for accepting each other as equals in the team.

'Ferrari is the myth of Formula 1.
The tradition, the soul, the passion.'

Ayrton Senna

7
FERRARI F1
A culture of champions

Sunday, 13 October 2002,
Suzuka, Japan

The seventeenth and final round of the 2002 Formula 1 season is the Japanese Grand Prix. To underscore the Ferrari team's superlative season, Michael Schumacher begins the race in pole position, records the fastest lap and takes the chequered flag. He has made the podium in every round of the championship, coming either first or second, with only one third place, in Malaysia. With a total of 144 points, Schumacher is world champion by a record 67 points from the nearest contender, his own Ferrari teammate Rubens Barrichello. In fact, Schumacher had wrapped up the title at the French Grand Prix with six rounds to go. Ferrari, having won fifteen out of the seventeen rounds, with twenty-seven podium finishes, take the Constructors' Championship by an even greater margin – on 221 points, as many as all the other teams' points combined.

The comprehensive and emphatic dominance of Ferrari in the 2002 F1 season led to many fans claiming that the sport had lost its competitive magic, the normal cut and thrust of racing replaced by predictable Ferrari wins. But such dominance was not easily achieved or, in fact, predictable. It was forged out of an audacious vision and a master plan to build a dream team that took the best part of a decade of relentless effort to realize.

The oldest team in Formula 1, having competed in the first Formula One World Championship in 1950 and in every championship since, Ferrari had built a reputation in motor sport by producing great cars and turning out equally great driving champions such as Alberto Ascari in the early 1950s, Juan Manuel Fangio in 1956 and Niki Lauda in the 1970s. Passion for the *cavallino rampante*, Ferrari's black horse on yellow shield logo, had become global, but was especially intense in Italy, home to their fanatical supporters, the *tifosi*.

During the 1980s and much of the 1990s, however, Formula 1 was dominated by the technical brilliance and modern management logic of British-based teams such as Williams, Benetton and McLaren. Scuderia Ferrari, as the Formula 1 racing team is known, had become mired in political infighting, unnecessary bureaucracy and a loss of focus that meant creativity and flair rarely resulted in technical innovation. Combined, these factors produced cars in which not even great driving talent could succeed. Alain Prost, a four-time Formula 1 world champion, famously described his 1991 Ferrari as 'a pig' and 'an accident waiting to happen'. Nor did

Nigel Mansell, Jean Alesi or Gerhard Berger, all blisteringly quick racing drivers, fare much better.

By the mid-1990s it had been almost twenty years since Ferrari had won either the Drivers' World Championship or the Constructors' Championship. As Timothy Collings, long-time F1 reporter and author of *Formula One*, put it, 'Ferrari was a prancing horse with a pronounced limp.'

The journey from a limping horse to the almost flawless season in 2002 is the story of the development of a classic superteam: attracting great talent, integrating it effectively and developing a shared culture of excellence.

Assembling the talent

The renaissance of Ferrari as a force in Formula 1 can be traced back to 1991 when Luca di Montezemolo returned to Ferrari as President and Managing Director. Di Montezemolo had first joined Ferrari in 1973 as an assistant to Enzo Ferrari. The founder of the Ferrari brand had first noticed the young lawyer when he phoned a radio show to defend the Ferrari team, combining an articulate style with a passion for the marque. Di Montezemolo became team manager for the Ferrari F1 department in 1974 and went on to secure two Formula 1 Drivers' World Championships with Niki Lauda in 1975 and 1977, before moving on to run other areas within the Agnelli and Fiat empire.

Di Montezemolo continued to gain valuable experience and overcome significant challenges in the business of sport, spearheading Italy's first foray into the America's Cup, the Azurra Challenge, and then successfully running the FIFA World Cup finals as head of the host nation in Italia '90.

For Ferrari, di Montezemolo was an ideal leader. He shared the passion of the most ardent *tifoso*, but also understood the commercial importance of the relationship between a resurgent Formula 1 team and his performance-car business. Perhaps most importantly, in balancing his love for the team with his business acumen, di Montezemolo realized that significant change was needed to reignite the tradition of winning at Ferrari. He entrusted this critical mission to Jean Todt.

As with many things in Formula 1, Bernie Ecclestone, the architect of the modern sport, had a hand in bringing Todt to the role of Sporting Director at Ferrari in 1993. Ecclestone had recognized Todt's potential benefit to Ferrari and therefore, naturally, to Formula 1 as a whole. Todt had an impressive pedigree in motor sport, combining a successful career initially as a rally co-driver and an even more important period developing and leading a winning Peugeot-Talbot racing division that had dominated the World Rally Championship during the mid-1980s and won the Le Mans 24-Hour sports car race in both 1992 and 1993. Ecclestone and di Montezemolo recognized in the Frenchman someone capable of taming the politics at the Italian company and able to systematically construct a team that could return Ferrari to its former glories.

Todt and di Montezemolo focused not just on winning a

few races, but on carrying the spirit of Enzo Ferrari onwards into a new millennium. Theirs was a crusade to reinstate Ferrari as Formula 1's leading team. As Todt saw it, the crusade would be victorious in clear phases: from finishing the race and being in the top six, to being competitive and in contention, to establishing a dominant position.

They were prepared to take the existing Ferrari tradition and not be burdened by the history. They were ready to reinvent the tradition to reinforce it, to pay homage to it and yet renew it, to adapt and not jettison. They would figure out what needed changing and then proceed to implement that change systematically.

> 'You must make sure that you're always going in the right direction. You need to have people very focused on the medium- and long-term programmes as well as on daily programmes to make sure you don't lose direction.'
>
> Jean Todt

Just as they were united in their philosophical approach, Todt and di Montezemolo were also on the same page commercially. They saw that budgets were fundamental to success in the sport so their first objective was to secure a major sponsor to deliver the resources necessary to win. For tobacco giant Philip Morris, the opportunity to create Scuderia Ferrari Marlboro, with the branding potential of the common red colours and the chance to associate with the legendary Italian team, proved too attractive to ignore. The added financial muscle that the deal gave Ferrari enabled Todt to progress on the most critical move for the rebirth of the team.

Todt knew the essential step was to secure the right talent, and no one was more important in his eyes than the best driver. Initially Todt focused on the legendary Ayrton Senna. The triple Formula 1 world champion was, at the time, earning $1 million a race with McLaren in a deal that allowed him to leave at any time. Despite professing a desire to drive with Ferrari, 'even if their car was slower than a Volkswagen Beetle', the charismatic Brazilian wanted to win championships immediately and chose instead to join the dominant Williams-Renault team, rather than investing the two to three years that would be required to rebuild the Italian team to competitiveness.

Undeterred, Ferrari turned to Senna's emerging rival, Michael Schumacher. Schumacher's abilities as a racing driver had been quickly established and sealed in his two world championship titles with Benetton-Renault. Following the tragic death of Ayrton Senna during the 1994 San Marino Grand Prix at Imola, where Roland Ratzenberger also died, Schumacher was widely acknowledged as the fastest driver on the grid.

On arrival at Ferrari Schumacher's success was immediate. Despite the car still being broadly unimproved he managed to secure three victories in 1996, demonstrating the value of his record-breaking $24-million-a-year contract.

However, Schumacher had not joined Ferrari just to win

individual races. He craved further championship titles and relished the opportunity to rebuild Ferrari's mythical status. He quickly began to demand a different car design, one that better suited his driving style and that technically would ultimately have to outperform all competitors. To answer his wish, Todt and Schumacher turned to Ross Brawn and Rory Byrne.

The combination of Brawn, Schumacher and Byrne had already been successful. Together since the early 1990s, the trio had won two Drivers' and one Constructors' World Championship at Benetton. The lure of working with Schumacher again and the chance to revive the Ferrari legend was too great for Brawn and Byrne, and both joined the team in 1997.

Ross Brawn, then as now, was widely regarded as a master strategist. He had a holistic vision for what a winning car needed to be, able to conceive of and articulate what the complete package should look like and break it down into an integrated development plan for each of the myriad pieces. On race days he also had an unrivalled ability to determine the right strategy: the winning mix of fuel, tyres and pit stops to make the most of the car and the driver, given the specific challenges of the track and weather on the day and the competitive threat from other teams.

> 'Ross, because he is English, was the ideal bridge between the Italians, with their spaghetti culture, and Schumacher, with his German efficiency.'
> Niki Lauda

Rory Byrne was one of the leading car designers of his generation, his success largely the result of his meticulous perfectionism. During qualifying he would hold back the cars from their fast laps, waiting for a cloud to move across the sun, calculating that the small change in the ambient temperature would better suit the car and ensure an extra performance edge.

Todt also recognized that having a number of trusted colleagues whom he already knew well would be helpful in accelerating the team's performance: he brought in former winning colleagues from Peugeot, including Christophe Mary and Gilles Simon, who designed the all-conquering Ferrari V-10 engine.

Often considered the last and least member of an F1 team is the second driver. Playing a publicly clear second fiddle to a double world champion on whom the team is banking to reverse their fortunes is rarely the aspiration of ambitiously competitive Formula 1 racing drivers. A number of candidates were too proud to accept the role of supporting Michael Schumacher and in other instances the politics of asking an Italian driver to be number two to a German number 1 at Ferrari – the de facto Italian national team – was deemed unacceptable.

Eddie Irvine was driving for the rival Jordan racing team when, during a chance encounter and in his inimitable style, he cheekily asked Luca di Montezemolo for a discount on spares for his personal Ferrari road car. Di Montezemolo mused that the driver with the number 1 mouth might make a great number 2 driver.

The Northern Irishman Irvine was a hugely self-confident individual, a self-confessed playboy, but someone who knew his way round a racetrack. Jean Todt duly signed him up, recognizing his mental toughness and his capacity to cope with the particular pressures of being a number 2 driver. (Rubens Barrichello subsequently replaced Irvine as Schumacher's number 2 in 2000.)

More than individual talent – co-ordinating talent

While each of the recruits had obvious individual skills to contribute, the success of the team relied on the combination of these diverse skills.

One of the first actions Ross Brawn and Rory Byrne took was to unify the chassis design facilities and engine development under one roof, which under predecessor John Barnard had been split between Maranello in Italy and facilities in the UK. Bringing these groups together in close physical proximity enabled the team to work in a faster and seamless fashion. Brawn saw his role as creating the right environment, providing the means for others to achieve their objectives and get the job done.

Compared to the overlaps and gaps that had recently characterized the team, Brawn moved Ferrari towards a cleaner organizational structure, with clarity of individual roles and responsibilities balanced by a focus on the interface and co-ordination of different divisions. The epitome of this clarity could be seen in the pit stops, often the difference between winning and losing races.

A good pit stop comprised six or seven seconds of intense activity, during which the driver had to stop in precisely the right place for a team of mechanics to jack up the car, unbolt the wheels, replace them with fresh ones, add more fuel (a procedure outlawed today as too dangerous) and lower the car for the driver to drive safely away.

Ferrari applied a scientific and rigorous approach to defining the right co-ordination and choreography for the pit stop, based on a time-and-motion study on steroids. Everything the twenty mechanics did in the pit stop was captured and planned out on a single sheet of A4 in a flow chart, and then measured, refined, and practised over and over again to ensure the effective speed and safety of the procedure. Under Brawn and Todt, this discipline extended beyond the racing, into all areas of the team's efforts.

> 'I think the improvements you see
> and the reliability we make is through
> a way of work, a method.'
>
> Paolo Martinelli, Ferrari F1 engine designer

This attention to detail even went beyond Formula 1 when McLaren and Ferrari re-engineered the patient handover procedure following intensive cardiac operations on children at the Great Ormond Street Hospital using similar principles.

Professor Martin Elliott, the head of cardiac surgery at the Great Ormond Street Hospital for Children, said, 'The handover is perhaps the most critical stage of the operation, and a year or two ago it would have been full of noise and movement as everyone, including me, got into the action, often getting in each other's way, but that was before our research work with Ferrari transformed the way we work.'

As Nigel Stepney, then Ferrari's race technical director, explained, 'It takes a long time to establish a team. We have twenty-odd people working together for four to six years to get a routine which lasts little more than four seconds. They work round the clock, every day, with ever-changing personnel, so what they need is a formula to work to.'

As important as his decisive input to race strategy, Ross Brawn's contribution to the team was as an organizer. He deployed systematic approaches to clarifying the right processes, roles and responsibilities, synthesizing the formula for maximizing the contributions of the team members.

> 'The race is the icing on the cake. If the ingredients and the baking are no good then we're wasting our time.'
> Ross Brawn

This approach, one shared by Jean Todt, could also be seen in the many debriefings before and after each testing, practice and qualifying session, as well as in the race itself. In the past, under the immense pressures and expectations of working for Ferrari, the team had been mired in division and blame, rather than learning lessons from mistakes and failures. Adopting an approach similar to that of the military, the team used a disciplined protocol to explore what had happened, looking for the root causes and identifying areas of learning and making the necessary changes. A key facet of the success for the Ferrari team became their ability to learn from each experience and in particular use failure as a stepping stone towards success.

Communication and respect

Michael Schumacher is well known for his natural driving skills. Less well known is his ability to communicate effectively and motivate the rest of the team. Schumacher had the ability not only to drive quick laps but also to memorize and retain information on exactly how the car behaved at every point on the track and through each corner.

Sir Jackie Stewart, himself a triple world champion, reflects on the importance of such an ability. 'The hot-headed Young Turk can wring extra speed out of the car, but it usually doesn't last. Sustainable consistency is achieved by a driver who develops an ability to feel his car and becomes able to consume and then accurately reiterate these dynamic motions in a vivid and precise explanation to his engineer.'

A modern Formula 1 car has over 120 sensors on it that provide real-time measurement and data on the car's performance.

The analysis of this data is greatly enhanced by what Sir Jackie calls a driver's 'accurate subjective judgement'. With his deep understanding of mechanical engineering, intense curiosity and focus on improvement, Michael Schumacher became a master of communicating with his engineer to diagnose issues and prescribe solutions for improving the car.

A well-designed and engineered car amplified Schumacher's innate talent for speed. Equally, his ability to understand and communicate the performance of the car amplified his technical team's ability to improve it. Success was the result of a partnership that multiplied the strengths of both partners. Similarly, Brawn was also able to exploit Schumacher's laser focus and his ability to drive consistently fast lap times on demand to compute race tactics with a level of precision and foresight that delivered victories.

These partnerships between driver and engineer, and between driver and race strategist, were amongst the many 'working marriages' that defined the Ferrari team. As with all successful collaborations, the central tenet was mutual respect.

Respect for other team members was something that Jean Todt turned into a culture at Ferrari, leading by example with his own behaviour. 'Sometimes people in Formula 1 are very arrogant. But I think that in the way that you lead your life, even if you are very determined and have big ambitions, you must be very humble. You must try to make yourself available for others.'

Schumacher, too, shared this feeling deeply. While

other drivers played mere lip service to this team ethic – an approach that rarely made it past anyone's bullshit detectors – Schumacher genuinely lived it. After every victory, having received the trophy and sprayed the traditional champagne from the podium, Schumacher's first subsequent action was to individually thank and shake the hand of each team member in the garage. Steve Matchett, a mechanic when Schumacher was at Benetton, later reflected on the impact of this show of appreciation from a world champion: 'I have never felt such an integral part of a team than when I worked with Michael.' More tellingly, perhaps, Schumacher also shook hands with the entire garage when he *lost* a race.

It was an approach that extended to Ferrari's technical partners, as Hiroshi Yasukawa of Bridgestone tyres explained. 'The people at Ferrari tried hard to understand the Japanese mentality. Not only Jean Todt and Michael Schumacher, but throughout Ferrari, everyone tried to understand our way of working and even our way of living.'

The winners brought together at Ferrari were distinctive in their collective appreciation of the commitment and effectiveness of every single team member. Underpinning the Ferrari approach was a shared philosophy that they could only win together as a unit and that every team member had a critical role to play. The philosophy that no one worked for themselves, that they all worked for Ferrari, was continuously reinforced with the 750 who worked as part of the community at Gestione Sportiva.

> 'It is something we tell them all the
> time – that they are an intrinsic and
> vital part of the success of Ferrari.'
>
> Ross Brawn

Attitude and hard work

The family feeling, the sense of community, at Ferrari should not, however, be mistaken for a lack of edge. Jean Todt had built a team committed to the business of winning. The desire to compete and win provided an inner steel that sharpened the team's performance and its relentless pursuit of improvement. At its best it was an urge to discover more, a curiosity and will to continue getting better, often the mark of champions.

Michael Schumacher expressed his own version of this: 'The feeling of being on the borderline, of developing one's potential, of constantly pushing back the limits. That's what keeps me motivated.'

In addition to the sense of honour and obligation of working for Ferrari, and in conjunction with mutual respect and commitment, the will to win provided a further boost to the effort the team would put in. In the end, much of the team's success came down to application and intensity. The attitude had to be right for the demanding work rate necessary to win.

> 'The magic of Ferrari is outside.
> Inside there is no magic of Ferrari.
> We just have to work.'
>
> Jean Todt

Schumacher, Brawn and Todt were all famous for living the job and much of the performance during races was the result of the systematic and tireless efforts of the whole team behind the scenes. The drive for victory could also be seen in the preparedness to improve the team. Todt moved on from the fans' favourites Jean Alesi and Gerhard Berger as soon as Michael Schumacher committed, and from successful designer John Barnard as soon as Rory Byrne and Ross Brawn could join. Having replaced Eddie Irvine, who left to be lead driver at the newly formed Jaguar team, Brawn was also quick to switch his allegiance to Rubens Barrichello. 'I think Rubens has done more for us in four races than Eddie did in three years,' was his assessment.

In the competitive 'Piranha Club' world of Formula 1, victory was sweeter as it meant competitors also lost. In building the team, Todt also weakened his competitors, luring Schumacher and then Brawn from Benetton (Byrne had officially retired). In establishing long-term partnerships with Shell, Bridgestone and Philip Morris he deprived McLaren of key technical and financial resources.

The desire to win was so powerful, though, that it sometimes strayed over the line into the dark side. Most infamous was the incident in the final race of the 1997 season at Jerez, when Schumacher, leading the championship by a single point from Jacques Villeneuve, deliberately crashed into his rival in an attempt to prevent him winning the championship. The plan backfired spectacularly. Not only was Schumacher's Ferrari too badly damaged to continue as Villeneuve finished third to take the title, but the German was also stripped of all the points he had won during the season. It was an action that has tainted his reputation ever since.

Equally controversial were Ferrari's team orders during the 2002 Austrian Grand Prix, which saw Barrichello cede his winning position to Schumacher to secure maximum points for the German in his charge for the Drivers' Championship. For many fans, this was anathema, against all the natural laws of competitive racing. For Ferrari, however, it was a prime example of the team taking precedence over the individual.

For Todt and Brawn, even the bad years were team-building opportunities, and they exploited the adversity and disappointment to fuel the camaraderie and sense of determination in the team. When victory finally returned to Ferrari it was no fluke. It was the disciplined execution of a plan to build and develop a high-performance team fuelled by a common purpose.

The blueprint for the dominance of the 2002 season had been laid almost a decade beforehand. By 2003, ten years after Jean Todt's appointment, the Ferrari F1 team had won five consecutive Constructors' Championships and Schumacher four Drivers' Championships. Sales of new Ferrari cars rose from 2,289 in 1993 to nearly 6,500 in 2007. The superteam had achieved their dream of revitalizing the Ferrari legend.

> 'It is a result of having most of the people here who are leaders in their field. They have a common vision, a common understanding of things. They suffered together, resisted together.'
>
> Jean Todt

TEAM TALK Adapt or die

Ferrari's journey from limping horse to leaping stallion offers a road map for change that other teams can follow to transform their own performance.

Ferrari had a long heritage of success. It was the team most associated with the sport of Formula 1 motor racing. The team had epitomized Italian flair, design, performance and craftsmanship backed by the exuberant passion of the *tifosi*. Over time, however, these ingredients that had once combined to create the legend had become fragmented. After the death of Enzo Ferrari, the team was deeply divided and passion led mainly to long-running and vicious arguments rather than victory. A team divided by politics was also divided physically, with John Barnard in England separated from the rest of the team in Italy. The results of these divisions and the lack of teamwork were apparent in the car. Unreliable and slow compared to Williams and McLaren, Ferrari were uncompetitive across nearly every aspect of the sport.

It was evident that change was needed. Staying the same, doing the same things in the same ways, but hoping for different results was not a viable alternative. In charting the course back to the top, the Ferrari team forged a clear and compelling common purpose.

The starting point of every team journey is a shared ambition. All members of the Ferrari team were already winners in Formula 1. Individual victories and even single championships were not enough to attract or motivate them. The team was fuelled by the common purpose of revitalizing the Ferrari legend. Living up to the spirit of Enzo Ferrari was their holy grail, translated on to the track: the team sought total victory, total dominance.

Driving ever forward

Given the previous two decades of disastrous results, there was no question that their shared purpose was an audacious goal, one worthy of the full commitment of the team, all of whom could have taken easier and less risky paths to success. The challenge of rebuilding and perhaps even surpassing former glories made joining and staying at Ferrari compelling; it was a true test of champions.

The team understood that success would be based on the effective integration of the various elements of a Formula 1 car – the tyres, the engine, the chassis, the aerodynamics – as well as race strategy. A winning car is the product of the team of technical specialists, designers, engineers and mechanics and – of course – the driver. The full package is needed simply to compete. Winning was absolutely a team game.

The team at Ferrari also developed a realistic assessment of their starting position and were clear about what they had to change. There was no question they would need a more reliable and faster car, and of course they would need to inject new team members, not least a new lead driver. They were agreed that to reverse the team's fortunes they would have to address deeply embedded causes of failure, including replacing the company's political and divided culture with teamwork.

There were also elements that they needed to preserve, build on and even amplify, for example the power of the passion and the Ferrari tradition present in many of the existing team members as well as the *tifosi*. They understood that they needed to maintain and grow parent company Fiat's deep-pocketed support, as well as acknowledging that they would need access to more funds.

Having undertaken a robust analysis of their current position and decided on a clear direction, the team developed a shared road map for the journey ahead. For Todt the map was a blueprint for success: the team composition and the team culture. For Brawn the map had to deliver his vision of the complete car capable of winning everything. It required campaigns to revamp the chassis, the engine, the tyres, the aerodynamics and the fuel and lubricants.

For both the map was a holistic view of how all of these components would work together. Their shared skill was in developing and communicating a compelling definition of victory as well as breaking that goal down into smaller, achievable milestones. And for the rest of the team at Ferrari it provided a shared understanding of where they were starting from and a commitment to where they were going and by which route.

Investing in the *right* resources

Di Montezemolo and Todt's first steps were to find the resources necessary to fulfil Ferrari's purpose. They started by securing strong commitment from the parent company and more powerful sponsors. They set Ferrari up for success, and were well aware of the snowball effect it would create: winning would gain more prize money and an increased share of TV revenues, which in turn would lead to more successes and even more resources. Their strategy set out to master Formula 1's winner-take-all model of competition. The execution of their plan led to the unrivalled dominating run of success. By the early 2000s Ferrari's F1 team had the largest budget at just over $300 million a year, when the average was nearer

$200 million, and two wind tunnels, enabling twice the amount of aerodynamic testing compared to their competitors.

No team can deliver superior results on a sustainable basis without the right resources. Resources are not, however, enough to transform perennial losers into all-conquering champions. Toyota invested over $3 billion in their Formula 1 team from 2002 to their withdrawal in 2010. While company president Akio Toyoda cited the global financial crisis as the reason for their exit, Toyota's decision would have been based on the team's systematic failure to turn the resources into race results. Toyota enjoyed one of the largest budgets in Formula 1 history but failed to register a single Grand Prix victory.

Toyota, despite the vast investment, never truly committed to Formula 1. Instead the F1 team was treated as a marketing exercise. Racing at this level of competition was not part of their purpose or soul, a clash with a culture more suited to being the most successful mass producer of quality cars.

Ferrari demonstrate that teams going from zeroes to heroes need to do more than spend money. They need to change critical team members, to review their approach to collaboration and to embed the change into a new team culture. Given the central importance of talent in determining team success, and given the size of the change needed, it is no surprise that Ferrari's transformation started by replacing some key personnel. With di Montezemolo, Todt, Schumacher, Brawn and Byrne in place, Ferrari had a powerful coalition to drive the change.

Each member of this team was either the undisputed best or, at worst, in the top two in their field. The team had an undeniable track record of success in motor sport and knew what it would take to win future championships. What also made the new additions stand out was their shared understanding and acknowledgement of the fundamental nature of teamwork in Formula 1. Team conscientiousness is what separates individual champions from those who can be part of a winning team. The critical difference is that they have a deeply held belief that teamwork is essential to their own success, that they cannot win unless the team does.

Michael Schumacher epitomized these qualities. He drove for himself and the team. His relentless testing and his ability to communicate how the car was performing were essential advantages to the team. He demanded great teammates and when things went wrong he was harder on himself than he was on them. In many ways he was a role model for the team behaviour Ferrari needed. Indeed, there are those who see his achievements and those of Scuderia Ferrari as more a product of his team spirit and team-building skills than his driving.

Sir Jackie Stewart was also a team player as well as being a fast driver, winning three World Championships in 1969, 1971 and 1973. He has always been the first to acknowledge the importance of the team around him, stating that his life depended on his mechanics and his success on the leadership of Ken Tyrrell. His mechanics were inspired by his speed and smooth driving, pointing out his remarkable success in winning 25 per cent of all of his F1 races. He showed them equal respect in return, firm in his requests but never aggressive. Symbolic touches, similar to Schumacher's handshakes after races, such as dinners with his mechanics in Monaco and rides around the racetracks in a Volkswagen Beetle, had a powerful effect on team morale and cohesion.

Neil Davis was part of the Tyrrell team from 1960 to 1998. 'The thing about Jackie was that you wanted to achieve things for him – he was always very calculating, knew exactly what he wanted from you and the car, and if you gave it to him you just knew he would go out there and win. I never wanted to work for any other team.'

Like Lionel Messi in football and Michael Jordan in basketball, Schumacher and Stewart were game-changing team members. Their teams could not win without them, but without teamwork throughout, the team could still lose.

Recruiting Schumacher early on in Ferrari's process of change was potent for a number of reasons. It provided an immediate performance impact on the track that gave the team hope that change was possible and worthwhile. The early success on the track gave the change process forward momentum. Bringing Schumacher in also sent a clear message to the rest of the team about the team's ambition and commitment to change. Schumacher's quality was undisputed; he could not, however, do the work of the hundreds of other members. The team was clear that it neither could nor should replace everyone; it wanted to build on the existing tradition and craftsmanship, infusing them with new focus.

The mechanics of team dynamics

As in the Formula 1 cars they build and race, a team is only as strong as its weakest component. The key to a fast car and a winning team is that each component or member of the team is great in their own way and also amplifies the performance of the other parts, enabling greatness around them. Schumacher epitomized the behaviours needed to be a great team member: working very hard to perform at his best, showing respect to other team members, supporting them as well as demanding high standards from them. Added to this was his ability to communicate effectively, to be able to identify the information others relied upon and to convey it quickly and precisely.

As a world champion and leader Schumacher's every action was monitored assiduously by the whole garage and factory. When he and the whole top team spoke with one voice and acted in unison their message was amplified further; it did not take long for their team-oriented behaviour to be imitated and adopted by everyone at Ferrari F1.

Changing key members changes the whole team. While leaders must constantly communicate the need for change and teamwork, it is everyday actions that speak louder than words.

Every Formula 1 car is a prototype. Although racing takes place on the weekend, the championship is often won through the speed of technological development that takes place throughout the year. Winning this race requires a scientific approach of rapid systematic experimentation, where innovations are planned, subjected to robust testing and review. The performance management loop of plan, do and review became a fundamental aspect of Ferrari's progress. Ross Brawn saw the need to embed a culture of continuous innovation at Ferrari. The renaissance in the racing team was not one big revolution but a systematic conveyor belt of improvements.

The review process, and in particular the focused follow-through, was the distinctive driver of the successful change. Ferrari implemented a disciplined process of review after testing, after every practice, after every qualifying session and after every race.

Taking to heart Napoleon Bonaparte's warning that 'the people to fear are not those who disagree with you, but those who disagree with you and are too cowardly to let you know', the reviews were deliberately designed to ensure hierarchy did not stop the flow of feedback. Because each team member had a contribution to make, the review sessions were so structured that everyone was actively involved, ensuring the team captured the breadth of perspectives. The review sessions started with expected or planned performance and then looked at areas where the results were either better or worse. Brawn understood that the key to unlocking a culture of innovation is to treat success and failure as equal sources of valuable data and the basis for learning to fuel further advances. The objective of reviews and feedback shifted to focus on learning to improve and away from the points scoring or passing the buck that had typified Ferrari's review process in the recent past.

The extensive data captured by the telemetry, the hundreds of measurements a second from throughout the engine, the suspension and the rest of the car, as well as information on the drivers' well-being, ensured that the discussions and exploration of what happened and why, were rich and objective. Passion was never too far from the surface, but it was no longer a game of pass the parcel of blame. It was a team effort to improve. This was constructive feedback, Formula 1 style.

While it was important to understand what had happened and to look at root causes, the bulk of the team's focus was on ensuring that lessons learned were quickly put into practice. The end of the review formed the beginning of the next planning session, with clearly defined actions linked to deadlines and accountability.

Ross Brawn championed this approach, initially driving it forward in person, calmly insisting on its execution through consistent repetition. As the team members became used to it, they understood it better and, importantly, as they began to see how it could help them and the team achieve its purpose, Brawn's systematic method became the norm.

Ferrari also worked hard at building a culture of teamwork. They approached collaboration between team members with the same application and discipline that they applied to developing and testing the car. Every team interaction was precision engineered. All key processes were mapped, tested and rehearsed, and based on feedback consequently re-engineered again in a continuous cycle. The desired team behaviours were clarified – who does what and when – and practised repeatedly. The pit stop is a case in point, with over twenty-one people involved in tightly co-ordinated action in a small space. Ferrari represented the pit stop visually on a single page, delivering simple clarity of team-member roles and interactions. With clarity in place the pit stop was practised over 2,000 times a year, ensuring wheel changes could be executed in under three seconds.

These new teamwork behaviours were imitated and adopted, fuelled by the growing success of the team, until they replaced the old divisive politics and became the 'way we do things around here', embedded as part of the team culture.

United by common purpose, Ferrari's culture exploited the diversity in the team. It blended Brawn's British scientific approach, Schumacher's Teutonic focus and Bridgestone's Japanese approach to partnership with an existing Italian passion and a lot of hard work.

The truth about building a new culture of teamwork is that it requires teams to focus and work at it. Teamwork is *hard* work. Defining the teamwork protocol together and then practising it over and over again creates a high-performance habit.

The teamwork that became the 'Ferrari way' never lost sight of the objective of winning. The aim was not just to build the team, the aim was to win. That performance edge was so strong that it occasionally let the ends dictate highly controversial means.

The strong team bonds formed were in the service of super-ior performance. Once the shared purpose was achieved and the legend had been revived, its unifying power was spent. The team fragmented, with each of the individuals moving off to find new crusades. When they stopped adapting to meet their shared goal, the team's domination stalled. Without the potent common purpose of reviving the Ferrari legend, it is difficult to see how the achievements of the Ferrari superteam can be repeated.

AGENDA Adapt or die

Excellence is a moving target and teams must constantly adjust their approach to stay ahead. The ability to change and improve is at the heart of building better teams.

Manage change – change management. If you are look-ing to change the way your team behaves, the most important place to start is by changing your own behaviour. Leaders in teams are role models and set the tone through their actions more than their words. Too much stress is placed on commu-nication campaigns, bright posters and long speeches when actually management itself is the message. Your actions will shape how others on the team behave; you can help the team become more supportive by being more supportive yourself. To be a catalyst, you need to be the first to change. One of the most powerful ways of changing your team is by changing its composition. Who you hire and promote reinforces the behaviours and attitudes that are embodied in those selected. When you dismiss a derailing team member it directly removes their negative contribution from the team, as well as sending a signal about behaviour that will not be tolerated. Combining the powerful impact of leadership and team composition, leaders reluctant to adapt should take heed: changing management may be the most potent form of change management.

Stay open to learning and be obsessive about improvement. At the heart of every great individual and team is the belief that they can get better. The team spirit you need to nurture is one of experimentation and excellence. This is an essential paradox of high performance, the need simultaneously to aim for excellence and acknowledge the importance of failure. Teams that aim to make no mistakes end up making nothing of consequence. You need to help your team accept that failure can teach you as much as success, and that it is a necessary step on the path to excellence.

Begin at the beginning. The first step in improving your team is to determine where the team currently is. Your team needs open and honest feedback to establish a clear and shared understanding of your current performance and the results it produces. Feedback based on good data is essential to help your team objectively face up to reality. This baseline will help you build the case for change and also give you the basis for diagnosing what needs to change.

Build the case for change. Your team will be driven by both hope and fear. Your common purpose should provide an inexorable pull and motivate the team to change for the better. Drawing out the fear and loathing that resides in crises, failures and losing to competitors can also motivate your team into action.

Dig for root causes. Once you are clear about what has happened you can begin to uncover why. Remember to focus equally on what worked and what didn't; look for best practices to expand on as well as correcting the problem areas. As you conduct a robust and rigorous review you need to guard against your team playing the blame game. Fear of being blamed and shamed in front of others can force team members to hide problems – untreated, they can often come back bigger and with more damaging consequences. Blame can also inhibit future performance, with teams playing not to lose and paralysed by fear of failure. Be sure to keep your team focused on the main aim: understanding the past to improve future performance.

Design the future together. The secret of delivering better performance lies in recognizing what can be done differently. The baseline and diagnosis are the warm-up acts, the focus on developing ideas and options for improving is the main event. The most powerful source of developing and executing new ideas and approaches for improving your team is . . . your team. Your team will have the closest experience of what works in practice and what doesn't. Involving them ensures that any change is not just theoretical but practicable. Getting your team to generate ideas also increases its ownership of the changes, especially compared to those tarnished with the stigma of 'not invented here'.

Focus on building new team norms. It is not enough to require improvements to how the team will operate. To achieve better results you will actually need to do things differently. There are four factors that most determine whether the changes you start will stick.

(1) Identify the few areas of teamwork with the greatest potential and choreograph tightly how the team will now interact, recasting role clarity with great precision. Use a scalpel rather than an axe. Try to avoid the wanton destruction of revolution and opt for more focused interventions that build on what is working and change only what is necessary. The aim is for a series of targeted improvements, the effects of which can be isolated and measured, so minimizing the scope for collateral damage.

(2) New approaches need to be trained and deliberately practised. Individuals learn best by doing and teams by doing together. Your team needs to rehearse the revised approach, again and again, until it becomes well honed and second nature.

(3) Most importantly the changes need to work. Your team will repeat and imitate examples of new behaviours that are proven to work in practice. The fastest way of getting your team to adopt a new way of behaving is for them to experience the benefits of the changed approach in terms of the results it achieves. Despite the undoubted power of communication, your team won't change just because you say it should. It is not enough that they hear about the change, they need to do it and to feel it.

(4) Finally, you can weave these new behaviours into the fabric of the team by recognizing them through rewards and crafting team stories that celebrate collective achievements. Over time and through repeated rehearsal and success, the shared approach will become a habit, part of the team culture, 'the way we do things around here'.

CONCLUSION
The protocols of performance

In *Superteams* I have sought to give readers inspiration and insight into some of the greatest teams in the world. I have also endeavoured to draw out guidelines for application by leaders and members of teams in all kinds of situations. Taken together, the seven core tasks provide a clear agenda for building better teams and delivering high performance.

Each of the teams explored in the book had forged a **clear and compelling common purpose**. For the team at Pixar it was inheriting Disney's legacy in the digital age. The British Red Cross was driven to mobilize humanity to save lives. For the Ryder Cup it was 14½ points. A set of shared objectives is the most potent force in attracting the right talent, getting them to want to do great work and to want to do it together.

All the teams in the book were well led. Rather than a single 'right' approach to **leading the team**, different situations and individuals require leaders to flex their style. Crisis can initially demand a direct, even autocratic approach, as the Red Cross demonstrated. In the Ryder Cup Colin Montgomerie had to lead without hitting a shot; instead he had the final say in selection and coached his players at moments of truth. In the Rolling Stones each member takes on a different role: Keith is the band's spiritual leader, Ronnie the chief mediator, Charlie is the backbone and backbeat and Mick is in control of everything he can be. Your team will be strongest when each member of the team takes ownership of inspiring, supporting and holding each other accountable: when the team is full of leaders.

All of the teams ensured they had the best possible members for their specific mission. Individual excellence remains central to performance. The SAS has developed a process that trains the best and discards the rest, isolating the essence of talent and testing for it ruthlessly. Ferrari's renaissance was based on attracting the best in every role. That was defined not just by individuals' technical skills but also by their multiplier effect on the rest of the team. Like Colin Montgomerie, you should aim to build a team of the 'best twelve', rather than the 'twelve best'. Individuals are the building blocks, so you need to **pursue a quest for the best**, selecting and developing the right calibre and mix of members.

The seven teams made every effort to create the conditions where their members were set up to succeed. The Red Cross faced the chaos of disaster by controlling everything they could: they pre-packaged resources in the emergency relief units and ensured every meeting had a clear agenda, with the right attendees and information. Where necessary, teams like Ferrari and Pixar negotiated and invented the resources they needed. All the teams knew that small details mattered, such as the diamond-shaped table in Northern Ireland and the Ryder Cup scoreboards at Celtic Manor. Teams **shape the environment for success**, ensuring the team is as small as possible, with clearly defined roles, the right resources and relationships that are fit for purpose.

Teams that succeed **build cohesion**. They stay glued to their task and stick together, even under pressure. The Rolling Stones share a common past, broad musical tastes and, most powerfully, a common purpose. They have grown to trust each other through success and survival. They have become a cohesive unit – and though active in a notoriously fickle business, they are the longest-lasting of all the seven superteams in this book. Teams who stay together over time tend to enjoy being together. Teamwork is often fun and fulfilling, even if it means needing time and space apart. Shared purpose and social bonds can reinforce cohesion and in doing so raise performance, especially when leavened with the occasional good fight.

Too much cohesion can lead to 'groupthink', when individual thought is stifled, and too much conflict to the team fragmenting. The Northern Ireland peace process demonstrated the need to neutralize fears and humanize adversaries to move beyond conflict. For the SAS absolute clarity on roles and their boundaries is a way of avoiding friendly fire. Pixar and the Stones, on the other hand, highlight the importance of keeping abrasion alive to provide sparks for creativity. **Mastering conflict** is essential to ensuring your team can be both creative and cohesive.

Finally, teams need the ability to change and continuously improve; teams need to **adapt or die**. The most powerful assets for changing 'the way we do things around here' are the team members themselves. Tony Blair and Mo Mowlam's arrival were strong signals of change in Northern Ireland. The uncomfortable truth is that you may have to change the membership of your team to drive change. Similarly, the new team at Ferrari embodied change and reinforced it by instilling a more scientific approach to complement the existing passion. They built a new culture by ensuring the team experienced the disciplined choreography working in practice and in victory. Where possible, ownership for developing new approaches should come from your own team: they will know what will work, and if involved they will be more committed to it. To cement that commitment, how you behave as the team leader, including who you recognize and reward, plays a fundamental role. In changing culture, management is the message.

The springboard

The teams in this book succeeded in their crucible moment because they had mastered the tasks of team-building and teamwork. They had developed their approaches into high-performance habits. Whether the Rolling Stones playing to an audience 'a mile long' on Copacabana Beach or the British Red Cross shifting gears to deal with disaster, each team invested time and effort in developing their own norms or protocols for performance.

So the final lesson is that you will need to tailor your own protocols for performance to fit your team's common purpose. In doing so, it is worth remembering that the essence of teamwork is hard work. There is no substitute for the ongoing commitment and continuous deliberate practice required to build better teams.

I hope that this book will serve both as a springboard and as a map to guide you. More tips, diagnostic tools and new case studies can be found at www.superteams.org. I look forward to using the space, to hearing your team stories and discussing how we can all engage in building better teams.

> 'Never doubt that a small group of thoughtful, committed citizens can change the world. Indeed, it is the only thing that ever has.'
>
> Margaret Mead, cultural anthropologist

ACKNOWLEDGEMENTS

This is a book about teams and is written standing on the shoulders of many giants. It is based on a privileged experience over the past twenty years of working with teams and exploring how they can work better. My special thanks to the following for their insight and inspiration: Sir Jackie Stewart, Colin Montgomerie, Ronnie Wood, Sir Nicholas Young and Bernie Shrosbree.

My thanks also to: Tristam Cones, William Gray, Anthony Bryans, Paul De Groot, James Hutton Mills, Rupert Sheehan, Jesse Wood, Jim Sturridge, Ekow Eshun, Helena Rohner, Mike Goldstein, Alex Thomas, Uli Weber, Claudia Galante, Rob Crabb, Nils Fluck, Dominic Sturridge, Ed Gray, Arthur De Groot, Ruth Lovering, Gordon Hughes, Liz Rayner, Peter Burns, Clive Mather, George Lefroy, Chris Knight, Michael Schumacher, Jean Todt, Chris Mathias, Gerald Chertavian, Michael Moore, Tim Critchley, Colin Gounden, Tessa Graham, Craig Kanarick, Lord Browne, Hesham Ezzat, Jamie Oliver, Mark Fuller, Joe Fuller, Waleed Iskandar, Jeffrey Rayport, Hanno Ronte, Mike Standing, Nikos Mourkogiannis, John

Viney, Martin Brundle, Lord Jacob Rothschild, Richard Rawlinson, Jake Leslie Melville, Alan Gemes, Shumeet Banerji, Professor Manfred Kets de Vries, Professor Elisabet Engellau, Professor Graham Ward, Professor George Kohlrieser, Professor Joachim Schwass, Ram Charam, Pat Williams, Professor Stuart Diamond, Nick Shannon, Patsy Rodenburg, Fran Griffiths, Steve Ward, Dan Einzig, Nick Mason, Alan Dunn, Lauren Ellis, Mike Goodhand, Mark South, Charles Williams and Philip Dodd, Joel Rickett, Richard Lennon, Jessica Jackson, James Scroggs, and especially Jane Pennyfather.

The first team is family. To my parents, Bac Muoi and sister Lan, who continue to give me the love and confidence to be myself.

This book is dedicated with all my love to Team Tu: Samantha, Maya, Louis and Amelie.

SELECTED
FURTHER READING

Chapter 1 Pixar

Bill Capodagli and Lynn Jackson, *Innovate the Pixar Way* (McGraw-Hill, 2010)

Ed Catmull, 'How Pixar Fosters Collective Creativity', *Harvard Business Review*, 2008

Malcolm Gladwell, 'Creation Myth', *New Yorker*, 16 May 2011

Pam Grady, 'It was love at first screening for Pixar Producer', *San Francisco Chronicle*, 13 June 2010

Harvard Business School (comp.), *Managing Creativity and Innovation* (Harvard Business School Press, 2003)

Laura M. Holson, 'John Lasseter: Disney's New Boss Reimagines the Magic Kingdom', *International Herald Tribune*, 5 March 2007

Walter Isaacson, *Steve Jobs* (Little, Brown, 2011)

Rick Lyman, 'A Digital Dream Factory in Silicon Valley', *New York Times*, 11 June 2001

John Markoff, *What the Dormouse Said: How the Sixties Counterculture Shaped the Personal Computer Industry* (Penguin, 2005)

Karen Paik, *To Infinity and Beyond!* (Virgin Books, 2007)

David A. Price, *The Pixar Touch* (Vintage Books, 2009)

Brent Schlender, 'Pixar's Magic Man', *Fortune*, 17 May 2006

William C. Taylor and Polly LaBarre, *Mavericks at Work* (HarperCollins, 2006)

Catherine Thimmesh, *Team Moon* (Houghton Mifflin, 2006)

Stefan Thomke and Barbara Feinberg, *Design Thinking and Innovation at Apple* (Harvard Business School Press, 2010)

Robert Velarde, *The Wisdom of Pixar* (InterVarsity Press, 2010)

David B. Yoffie and Renee Kim, *Apple Inc. in 2010* (Harvard Business School Press, 2010)

Chapter 2 European Ryder Cup Team 2010

The 2010 Ryder Cup Diary (European Tour for Lace DVD, 2010)

Ed Bradley, Tiger Woods interview on *60 Minutes* (CBS, 2006)

Iain Carter, *Monty's Manor* (Yellow Jersey Press, 2010)

Darren Clarke, *Heroes All* (Hodder and Stoughton, 2006)

Bruce Critchley, *The Captain's Challenge: Winning the Ryder Cup* (Icon Books, 2008)

Norman Dabell, *How We Won the Ryder Cup* (Mainstream Publishing, 2006)

Colin Montgomerie, *My Official Guide: Ryder Cup 2010* (Media Wales/European Tour, 2010)

Chapter 3 The SAS Iranian Embassy Siege Team

Michael Asher, *The Regiment: The Real Story of the SAS* (Penguin, 2008)

Mir Bahmanyar with Chris Osman, *SEALs: The US Navy's Elite Fighting Force* (Osprey Publishing, 2008)

Dick Couch, *The Warrior Elite* (Three Rivers Press, 2003)

Mike Curtis, *Close Quarter Battle* (Corgi, 1998)

Rusty Firmin and Will Pearson, *GO! GO! GO!* (Weidenfeld & Nicolson, 2010)

Robin Horsfall, *Fighting Scared: Para, Mercenary, SAS, Sniper, Bodyguard* (Cassell, 2002)

Jon E. Lewis (ed.), *SAS: The Autobiography* (Robinson, 2011)

Hugh McManners, *Ultimate Special Forces* (Dorling Kindersley, 2008)

Mike Morgan, *The SAS Story* (Sutton Publishing, 2008)

Chris Ryan, *Fight to Win* (Century, 2009)

Leroy Thompson, *The Counterterrorist Manual* (Frontline Books, 2009)

Chapter 4 The Red Cross in Haiti

Dan Bortolotti, *Hope in Hell: Inside the World of Médecins Sans Frontières* (Firefly Books, 2004)

Margie Buchanan-Smith with Kim Scriven, *Leadership in Action: Leading Effectively in Humanitarian Operations* (Active Learning Network for Accountability and Performance, June 2011, www.alnap.org/resource/6118.aspx)

Kevin M. Cahill, MD (ed.), *Emergency Relief Operations* (Fordham University Press/Center for International Health and Cooperation, 2003)

Emily Ford, 'Picking Up the Pieces when Disaster Strikes', *The Times*, 8 January 2010

George D. Haddow and Jane A. Bullock, *Introduction to Emergency Management* (Butterworth-Heinemann, 2008)

Eric James, *Managing Humanitarian Relief: An Operational Guide for NGOs* (Practical Action Publishing, 2008)

Sam Jones, 'Rescue Teams Fly in amid Dire Warnings from Aid Agencies', *Guardian*, 14 January 2010

Nadine Pequeneza, *Inside Disaster Haiti* (PTV Productions, 2010)

Save the Children, *An Independent Joint Evaluation of the Haiti Earthquake Humanitarian Response* (Save the Children/ Care and Emergency Capacity Building Project, October 2010)

Isak Svensson and Peter Wallensteen, *The Go-Between* (United States Institute of Peace, 2010)

Sally Williams, 'Recovery Position', *Daily Telegraph*, 27 February 2010

Chapter 5 The Rolling Stones

Robert Greenfield, *Exile on Main Street* (Da Capo Press, 2007)

———, *Stones Touring Party: A Journey Through America with the Rolling Stones* (Aurum Press, 2010)

Mick Jagger, Keith Richards, Charlie Watts and Ronnie Wood, *According to the Rolling Stones* (Weidenfeld & Nicolson, 2003)

Nick Mason, *Inside Out – A Personal History of Pink Floyd* (Weidenfeld & Nicolson, 2004)

Keith Richards, *Life* (Weidenfeld & Nicolson, 2010)

Andy Serwer, 'Inside the Rolling Stones Inc.', *Fortune*, 30 September 2002

Ronnie Wood, *Ronnie* (Pan Books, 2008)

Chapter 6 The Northern Ireland Peace Process

Gerry Adams, *Hope and History* (Brandon, 2003)

Tony Blair, *A Journey* (Arrow Books, 2011)

Alastair Campbell, *Diaries Volume Two: Power and The People* (Hutchinson, 2011)

Aaron Edwards and Cillian McGrattan, *The Northern Ireland Conflict* (Oneworld Publications, 2010)

Roger Fisher and Daniel Shapiro, *Building Agreement* (Random House Business Books, 2007)

Dean Godson, *Himself Alone* (HarperPerennial, 2005)

Julia Langdon, *Mo Mowlam: The Biography* (Little, Brown, 2000)

Eamonn Mallie and David McKittrick, *The Fight for Peace: The Secret Story Behind the Irish Peace Process* (William Heinemann, 1996)

——, *Endgame in Ireland* (Hodder and Stoughton, 2001)

Mo Mowlam, *Momentum* (Hodder and Stoughton, 2003)

Jonathan Powell, *Great Hatred, Little Room* (Vintage, 2009)

Chapter 7 Ferrari F1

James Allen, *Michael Schumacher: The Edge of Greatness* (Headline Publishing Group, 2007)

Timothy Collings, *The Piranha Club* (Virgin Books, 2001)

——, *Team Schumacher* (Highdown, 2005)

Nick Garton, *Cavallino Rampante: How Ferrari Mastered Modern-day Formula 1* (Haynes Publishing, 2003)

Mark Jenkins, Ken Pasternak and Richard West, *Performing at the Limit* (Cambridge University Press, 2005)

Michael Mack and Gerhard Steidl (eds), *Michael Schumacher* (Random House, 2003)

Steve Matchett, *The Mechanic's Tale* (Weidenfeld & Nicolson, 1999)

Jane Nottage, *Eddie Irvine: Life in the Fast Lane* (Ebury Press, 2000)

Stéphane Samson, 'Expressly Oriental', *F1 Racing*

Jackie Stewart, *Winning is not Enough* (Headline, 2007)

'Technology Transfer', *Race Tech Magazine*, October 2010

General

John Adair, *Effective Teambuilding* (Pan Books, 1987)

Chris Argyris, *On Organizational Learning* (Blackwell, 1994)

Winfred Arthur, Jr, Bryan D. Edwards, Suzanne T. Bell, Anton J. Villado and Winston Bennett, Jr, 'Team Task Analysis: Identifying Tasks and Jobs that are Team Based', *Human Factors: The Journal of the Human Factors and Ergonomics Society*, 2005

Oluremi B. Ayoko, Victor J. Callan and Charmine E. J. Härtel, 'The Influence of Team Emotional Intelligence Climate on Conflict and Team Members' Reactions to Conflict', *Small Group Research*, 2008

Warren Bennis and Patricia Ward Biederman, *Organizing Genius* (Perseus Books, 1997)

Ken Blanchard, *Leadership and the One Minute Manager* (HarperCollins, 2004)

Marije Bosch, Marjan J. Faber, Juliette Cruijsberg, Gerlienke E. Voerman, Sheila Leatherman, Richard P. T. M. Grol, Marlies Hulscher and Michel Wensing, 'Effectiveness of Patient Care Teams and the Role of Clinical Expertise and Coordination: A Literature Review', *Medical Care Research & Review*, 2009

John Browne, *Beyond Business* (Weidenfeld & Nicolson, 2010)

C. S. Burke, E. Salas, K. Wilson-Donnelly and H. Priest, 'How to Turn a Team of Experts into an Expert Medical Team: Guidance from the Aviation and Military Communities', *Quality and Safety in Health Care*, 2004

Ram Charan, *Boards that Deliver* (Jossey-Bass, 2005)

James C. Collins and Jerry I. Porras, 'Building Your Company's Vision', HBR *OnPoint*, 2000

Michelle M. Colman and Albert V. Carron, 'The Nature of Norms in Individual Sport Teams', *Small Group Research*, 2001

Petru L. Curseu, Patrick Kenis, Jörg Raab and Ulrik Brandes, 'Composing Effective Teams through Team Dating', *Organization Studies*, 2010

Marilyn Darling, Charles Parry and Joseph Moore, 'Learning in the Thick of It', *Harvard Business Review*, 2005

Carsten K. W. de Dreu, 'When too Little or too Much Hurts: Evidence for a Curvilinear Relationship between Task Conflict and Innovation in Teams', *Journal of Management*, 2006

Frédéric Delmar and Scott Shane, 'Does Experience Matter? The Effect of Founding Team Experience on the Survival and Sales of Newly Founded Ventures', *Strategic Organization*, 2006

Craig A. Depken II and Lisa E. Haglund, 'Peer Effects in Team Sports: Empirical Evidence From NCAA Relay Teams', *Journal of Sports Economics*, 2010

Christian Deutscher, 'The Payoff to Leadership in Teams', *Journal of Sports Economics*, 2009

Dennis J. Devine and Jennifer L. Philips, 'Do Smarter Teams Do Better? A Meta-Analysis of Cognitive Ability and Team Performance', *Small Group Research*, 2001

Peter Dodek, Renee Herrick and P. Terry Phang, 'Initial Management of Trauma by a Trauma Team: Effect on Timeliness of Care in a Teaching Hospital', *American Journal of Medical Quality*, 2000

Anne Donnellon, *Team Talk* (President and Fellows of Harvard College, 1996)

K. Anders Ericsson, Neil Charness, Paul J. Feltovich and Robert R. Hoffman (eds), *The Cambridge Handbook of Expertise and Expert Performance* (Cambridge University Press, 2006)

Kimberley L. Gammage, Albert V. Carron and Paul A. Estabrooks, 'Team Cohesion and Individual Productivity: The Influence of the Norm for Productivity and the Identifiability of Individual Effort', *Small Group Research*, 2001

David A. Garvin, *Learning in Action: A Guide to Putting the Learning Organization to Work* (Harvard Business School Press, 2000)

Ann Gilley and Steven J. Kerno, Jr, 'Groups, Teams, and Communities of Practice: A Comparison', *Advances in Developing Human Resources*, 2010

Stephen J. Guastello, 'Nonlinear Dynamics of Team Performance and Adaptability in Emergency Response',

Human Factors: The Journal of the Human Factors and Ergonomics Society, 2010

J. Richard Hackman, *Leading Teams* (Harvard Business School Press, 2002)

James Hardy, Mark A. Eys and Albert V. Carron, 'Exploring the Potential Disadvantages of High Cohesion in Sports Teams', *Small Group Research*, 2005

Rune Høigaard, Reidar Säfvenbom and Finn Egil Tønnessen, 'The Relationship between Group Cohesion, Group Norms, and Perceived Social Loafing in Soccer Teams', *Small Group Research*, 2006

Susan E. Jackson, Aparna Joshi and Niclas L. Erhardt, 'Recent Research on Team and Organizational Diversity: SWOT Analysis and Implications', *Journal of Management*, 2003

Saj-Nicole Joni and Damon Beyer, *The Right Fight* (HarperCollins, 2010)

Jon R. Katzenbach and Douglas K. Smith, *The Wisdom of Teams* (HarperBusiness Essentials, 1999)

D. Christopher Kayes, 'The 1996 Mount Everest Climbing Disaster: The Breakdown of Learning in Teams', *Human Relations*, 2004

Frank Kee, Tracy Owen and Ruth Leathem, 'Decision Making in a Multidisciplinary Cancer Team: Does Team Discussion Result in Better Quality Decisions?', *Medical Decision Making*, 2004

Manfred Kets de Vries, *The Leadership Mystique* (Pearson Education, 2006)

Cameron Klein, Deborah Diaz Granados, Eduardo Salas, Huy Le, C. Shawn Burke, Rebecca Lyons and Gerald F. Goodwin, 'Does Team Building Work?', *Small Group Research*, 2009

George Kohlrieser, *Hostage at the Table* (Jossey-Bass, 2006)

S. W. J. Kozlowski and B. S. Bell, 'Work Groups and Teams in Organizations', in W. C. Borman, D. R. Ilgen and R. J. Klimoski (eds), *Handbook of Psychology*, vol. 12: *Industrial and Organizational Psychology* (Wiley, 2003)

———, 'Group Learning', in V. I. Sessa and M. London (eds), *Team Learning, Development, and Adaptation* (Lawrence Erlbaum, 2008)

Steve Kozlowski and Daniel Ilgen, 'Enhancing the Effectiveness of Work Groups and Teams', *Psychological Science in the Public Interest*, 2006

Janice Langan-Fox, Sharon Code and Kim Langfield-Smith, 'Team Mental Models: Techniques, Methods, and Analytic Approaches', *Human Factors: The Journal of the Human Factors and Ergonomics Society*, 2000

Dorothy Leonard and Walter Swap, *When Sparks Fly* (Harvard Business School Press, 2005)

Kate Ludeman and Eddie Erlandson, 'Coaching the Alpha Male', *Harvard Business Review*, 2004

Michael Marquardt, Ng Choon Seng and Helen Goodson, 'Team Development via Action Learning', *Advances in Developing Human Resources*, 2010

Anju Mehta, Hubert Feild, Achilles Armenakis and Nikhil Mehta, 'Team Goal Orientation and Team Performance: The Mediating Role of Team Planning', *Journal of Management*, 2009

Eric Molleman, Manda Broekhuis, Renee Stoffels and Frans Jaspers, 'Consequences of Participating in Multidisciplinary

Medical Team Meetings for Surgical, Nonsurgical, and Supporting Specialties', *Medical Care & Research Review*, 2010

Richard Moore, *Sky's the Limit* (HarperSport, 2011)

Eileen Morley and Andrew Silver, 'A Film Director's Approach to Managing Creativity', *Harvard Business Review*, 1977

Nikos Mourkogiannis, *Purpose* (Palgrave Macmillan, 2006)

Dennis O'Connor and Leodones Yballe, 'Team Leadership: Critical Steps to Great Projects', *Journal of Management Education*, 2007

Michael E. Porter, *Competitive Strategy* (Free Press, 1980)
———, *Competitive Advantage* (Free Press, 1985)

Kathleen M. Propp, Julie Apker, Wendy S. Zabava Ford, Nancy Wallace, Michele Serbenski and Nancee Hofmeister, 'Meeting the Complex Needs of the Health Care Team: Identification of Nurse–Team Communication Practices Perceived to Enhance Patient Outcomes', *Qualitative Health Research*, 2010

Denise N. Rall, 'The "House that Dick Built": Constructing the Team that Built the Bomb', *Social Studies of Science*, 2006

Eduardo Salas, Diana R. Nichols and James E. Driskell, 'Testing Three Team Training Strategies in Intact Teams: A Meta-Analysis', *Small Group Research*, 2007

Eduardo Salas, Katherine A. Wilson, and C. Shawn Burke, 'Does Crew Resource Management Training Work? An Update, an Extension, and Some Critical Needs', *Human Factors: The Journal of the Human Factors and Ergonomics Society*, 2006

Paul M. Shelton, Alina M. Waite and Carole J. Makela, 'Highly Effective Teams: A Relational Analysis of Group Potency and

Perceived Organizational Support', *Advances in Developing Human Resources*, 2010

Amanuel G. Tekleab, Narda R. Quigley and Paul E. Tesluk, 'A Longitudinal Study of Team Conflict, Conflict Management, Cohesion, and Team Effectiveness', *Group & Organization Management*, 2009

Noel Tichy, 'No Ordinary Boot Camp', *Harvard Business Review*, 2001

Theresa M. Welbourne, Cynthia S. Cycyota and Claudia J. Ferrante, 'Wall Street Reaction to Women in IPOs: An Examination of Gender Diversity in Top Management Teams', *Group & Organization Management*, 2007

Pat Williams, *Extreme Dreams Depend on Teams* (Center Street, 2009)

Clive Woodward, *Winning* (Hodder and Stoughton, 2004)

Roland K. Yeo and Ursula E. Nation, 'Optimizing the Action in Action Learning: Urgent Problems, Diversified Group Membership, and Commitment to Action', *Advances in Developing Human Resources*, 2010

D. Kent Zimmerman and Scott R. Gallagher, 'Creativity and Team Environment: An Exercise Illustrating How Much One Member Can Matter', *Journal of Management Education*, 2006

PHILIP DELVES BROUGHTON

WHAT THEY TEACH YOU AT HARVARD BUSINESS SCHOOL

What *do* they teach you at Harvard Business School?

Graduates of Harvard Business School run many of the world's biggest and most influential banks, companies and countries. But what kind of person does it take to succeed at HBS? And would you want to be one of them?

For anyone who has ever wondered what goes on behind Harvard Business School's hallowed walls, Philip Delves Broughton's hilarious and enlightening account of his experiences on its prestigious MBA programme provides an extraordinary glimpse into a world of case-study conundrums, guest lectures, *Apprentice*-style tasks, booze luging, burn-outs and high flyers.

And with HBS alumni heading the very global governments, financial institutions and FTSE 500 companies whose reckless love of deregulation and debt got us into so much trouble, Delves Broughton discovers where HBS really adds value – and where it falls disturbingly short.

'Delves Broughton captures an essence of HBS that is part cult, part psychological morass, part hothouse . . . His book is invaluable. Quite brilliant'
Simon Heffer, *Literary Review*

'A funny and revealing insider's view . . . his fascination is infectious' *Sunday Times*

'A particularly absorbing and entertaining read' *Financial Times*

'Horrifying and very funny . . . An excellent book' *Wall Street Journal*

Bob Burg & John David Mann

THE GO-GIVER: A Little Story about a Powerful Business Idea

The Go-Giver tells the story of an ambitious young man named Joe who yearns for success. Joe is a true go-getter, though sometimes he feels as if the harder and faster he works, the further away his goals seem to be.

One day, desperate to land a big deal at the end of a bad quarter, he seeks advice from the enigmatic Pindar, a legendary consultant referred to by his devotees simply as the Chairman. Over the next week, Pindar introduces Joe to a series of 'go-givers' who teach Joe how to open himself up to the power of giving.

'Most people don't have the guts to buy this book, never mind the will to follow through and actually use it. But you do. And I'm certain that you'll be glad you did' Seth Godin, author of *The Dip*

'Not since *Who Moved My Cheese?* have I enjoyed a parable as much as this. You owe it to yourself to read *The Go-Giver* and share its message with those who matter most to you' David Bach, author of *The Automatic Millionaire*

'*The Go-Giver* is the best business parable since *The Greatest Salesman in the World* and *The One-Minute Manager*' Pat Williams, author of *Souls of Steel*, and senior vice president, Orlando Magic

GUY KAWASAKI

ENCHANTMENT: The Art of Changing Hearts, Minds and Actions

Enchantment

n: 1) To charm, delight, enrapture

How do companies such as Apple create such enchanting products? And how do some people always seem to enchant others?

According to bestselling business guru Guy Kawasaki, anyone can learn the art of enchantment. It transforms situations and relationships, turns cynics into believers and changes hearts and minds.

The book explains all the tactics you need to enchant. Kawasaki's lessons are drawn from his tenure at Apple, as well as his decades of experience as an entrepreneur. Few people in the world are more qualified to teach you how to enchant.

'The power of a really good idea to transform the marketplace and individual customer experiences is huge. Enchantment offers a wealth of insights to help businesses and entrepreneurs tap into that potential.' Sir Richard Branson, Founder of the Virgin Group

'Read this book to create a company as enchanting as Apple.' Steve Wozniak, co-founder of Apple

'Informative, concise guide from one of America's most influential and, yes, enchanting entrepreneurs.' *Kirkus*

SCOTT BELSKY

MAKING IDEAS HAPPEN: Overcoming the Obstacles Between Vision and Reality

Thomas Edison famously said that genius is 1% inspiration, 99% perspiration. Every day new solutions, revolutionary cures, and artistic breakthroughs are conceived and squandered by smart people. Along with the gift of creativity come the obstacles to making ideas happen: lack of organisation, lack of accountability and a lack of community support.

Scott Belsky has interviewsed hundreds of the most productive creative people and teams in the world, revealing one common trait: a carefully trained capacity for executing ideas. Implementing your ideas is a skill that can be taught, and Belshy distills the core principles in this book.

While many of us obsess about discovering great new ideas, Belsky shows why it is better to develop the capacity to make ideas happen - using old-fashioned passion and perspiration. *Making Ideas Happen* reveals the practical yet counterintuitive techniques of 'serial creatives' - those few who make their visions a reality.

'If you care about your art, your job or your market, you really have no choice but to read this book' Seth Godin, author of *Purple Cow and Linchpin*

'Ideas are easy. Implementation is hard. This book helps you with the hard part' Guy Kawasaki, former Apple guru and author of *The Art of the Start*

'This book is like a Swiss Army knife for ideas' Ji Lee, Creative Director at Google Creative Lab

'This is a book about execution, and when it comes to going from an idea to a real business, execution is everything' John Battelle, co-founder of *WIRED* and *BoingBoing*

RICHARD L. BRANDT

ONE CLICK: Jeff Bezos and the Rise of Amazon.com

Amazon's business model is deceptively simple: make online shopping so easy that customers won't think twice. It can be summed up by that button on every page: 'Buy now with one click'.

Why has Amazon been so successful? Much of it hinges on Jeff Bezos, the CEO and founder, whose unique character and ruthless business sense have driven Amazon relentlessly forward.

Through interviews with Amazon employees and competitors, *One Click* charts Bezos's rise from computer nerd to world-changing entrepreneur. It reveals how he makes decisions and where he will take Amazon next.

Amazon is a case study in how to reinvent an entire industry. It is one that anyone in business ignores at their peril.

'Richard Brandt compellingly profiles one of the great internet executives of the era' Stephen Leeb, author of *The Oil Factor* and *Red Alert*

'Meticulously researched and with breathless, pithy commentary. If you want to understand the Bezos phenomenon, this is an easy and efficient way to do it - just like shopping on Amazon.' *Management Today*

DAVID NOVAK

TAKING PEOPLE WITH YOU: The Only Way to Make Big Things Happen

You'll never accomplish anything big if you try to do it alone.

We all need people to help us along the way. If you want to start a business, launch a product, move your company in a new direction, or raise money for a good cause, you need help from your team.

Very few people get as much help from their team as David Novak. As the CEO of the world's largest restaurant company, with a staggering 1.4 million employees, he has spent the last ten years developing a program for creating effective leaders at every level.

In *Taking People With You*, he shows exactly how to keep your teams motivated and on track: never stop learning, always celebrate achievement and never tolerate poor performance.

'David Novak is the best at leadership, whether teaching it in this book or practicing it at Yum.' Warren Buffett, Chairman and CEO, Berkshire Hathaway

'An important book about motivation from a proven motivator.' Jack Welch, former Chairman and CEO, General Electric

'David Novak is a hard-driving CEO with a great heart and soul - and that gives him unique insight into both your own personal development and how to bring out the best in others....A leadership book you can actually use.' Jamie Dimon, Chairman and CEO, JPMorgan Chase

GEORGE ANDERS

THE RARE FIND: Spotting Exceptional Talent Before Everyone Else

How do venture capitalists pick winners like Apple? How do the FBI's hostage rescue team find agents for the world's toughest job? How do Hollywood casting agents and major sports scouts size up the best talent?

There's a huge difference between the very best performers and everyone else; in terms of productivity there's a five-to-one gap. No one can afford to settle for mediocrity. So how do talent scouts in every field identify genius and put it to work?

Talking to the world's best, most secretive talent scouts, George Anders found that they all share an intense belief in finding high achievers who can create big successes. These are the arenas where brilliant recruiting is most vital - and in *The Rare Find* Anders reveals how the rest of us can learn the hidden 'tells' that really matter.

Pairing these frontline observations with cutting-edge research from psychiatrists, economists, recruiters and business strategists, Anders shows how anyone can hone the ability to recognize future greatness and discover tomorrow's stars.

'George Anders finds the deep truth about choosing people right. You'll never make these supremely important decisions the same way again' Geoff Colvin, *author of Talent Is Overrated*

'George Anders combines deep reporting, vivid storytelling, and keen analysis to help unravel the mysteries of talent. Whether you're running a large organization or managing a small team, *The Rare Find* is that rare book - a must-read' Daniel H. Pink, author of *Drive* and *A Whole New Mind*

'Quite simply, the best book on the subject I've ever read' Daniel Coyle, author of *The Talent Code*